AF351373

CLAIRE HEARN

Lessons From The Boot

Personal Growth From Life In South Italy

Copyright © 2024 by Claire Hearn

All rights reserved. No part of this publication may be reproduced, stored or transmitted in any form or by any means, electronic, mechanical, photocopying, recording, scanning, or otherwise without written permission from the publisher. It is illegal to copy this book, post it to a website, or distribute it by any other means without permission.

First edition

This book was professionally typeset on Reedsy.
Find out more at reedsy.com

*To everyone that has ever crossed my path -
thank you for being my teacher.*

Contents

Introduction

The best thing about living in Italy is living in Italy.
The worst thing about living in Italy is living in Italy.

This book was originally going to be called *Minchia* (mink-key-ah), which is Sicilian dialect for any number of things, depending on who you speak to. It can be used to express delight - "Minchia I got the job!" or to express disgust, "I can't believe that happened. Minchia". If you decide to translate it - Minchia also refers to a part of the ahem, male anatomy. It's a word that sums up the many layers of Italian life.

When I left London to move to Italy in 2018, I thought I was ready. Little did I know what was to come. It turns out that Italy is a multifaceted country which has changed me beyond measure. I have undergone so much personal transformation, that I decided to share some of the lessons that I have learnt in a podcast of the same name, *Lessons from the Boot*. This collection of lessons taken from season one of the podcast series, documents what real Italy has taught me and not just the romanticised version, so often portrayed in films and books.

It turns out that I moved to a country which is more complicated than I could ever have imagined, yet in the strange twist of life, the best place

I could ever have relocated to.

I hope my words inspire, amuse and delight you - wherever you may be in the world.

1

Choosing Unhappiness

Do we choose to be unhappy?

It's an interesting question, isn't it? Happiness is something we all crave. We spend our lives chasing it, often in different ways and through various means. What if, in some cases though, people are actually *choosing* to be unhappy? What if this unhappiness is not just a byproduct of circumstances but rather a conscious—or maybe even unconscious—decision?

Think about it. We all know someone who seems perpetually dissatisfied with life. They might feel stuck in a job that doesn't pay well, trapped in a life lacking direction or burdened by loneliness. It's easy to recognise these feelings in others and perhaps, if we're honest, in ourselves too. Here's the real question though: What have they done about it? What have you done about it?

More often than not, the answer is *nothing*. Many people simply talk about their dissatisfaction and their unhappiness, without taking any meaningful action to change their situation. This is where the idea of unhappiness as a choice comes into play. As strange as it sounds, there's a certain comfort in feeling unhappy. It's familiar. It's a place we know well and even if we don't like it, there's a security in its predictability.

In Gay Hendricks' insightful book, *The Big Leap*, he introduces the concept of the "upper limit." This idea suggests that each of us has a personal threshold for happiness, a limit to how much joy, satisfaction and fulfilment we can comfortably handle. When life begins to exceed this threshold—when we start to feel happier than we're used to—it can be unsettling. Without realising it, many people self-sabotage, bringing themselves back down to their comfort zone, to the level of happiness— or unhappiness—they're used to.

What's fascinating is that this upper limit is different for everyone. For some, it's set low, allowing only small doses of happiness. For others, it's a bit higher. Here's the kicker: this limit isn't something we're born with. It's often set during our upbringing, shaped by the circumstances and environments we grew up in. So, when you think about it, there's no universal level of happiness that fits all. We each have our own, deeply personal comfort level.

Now, let's dig a little deeper. If we're choosing to be unhappy, why would we do that? The answer often lies in our fear of change. Change is scary. It requires us to step out of our comfort zones, to take risks and to venture into the unknown. For many, this prospect is paralysing. Instead of embracing the possibility of something better, we retreat into excuses: "It's not possible for me because of X, Y, and Z," or "The system is rigged against people like me."

These excuses, however valid they may seem, are a way of avoiding the truth. The truth is that we're choosing to remain where we are, choosing to stay within the boundaries of our upper limit, because it feels safer. We convince ourselves that change is impossible, that happiness is out of reach and in doing so, we choose a life of lack over a life of abundance.

Living in South Italy, I see this dynamic play out often. Life here isn't easy—there's poverty and there's a lack of opportunities. Beyond the challenges, there's also a resignation, a surrender to the way things are. It's as if people have given up, accepting unhappiness as their lot in life. Is it really the circumstances that keep them down, or is it their choice to accept those circumstances without seeking change?

Everything in life is a choice. Our happiness, our sadness, our progress in our careers, the creativity we express, our relationships—all of it stems from the choices we make. Yet, so many of us give away our power, blaming external factors for our dissatisfaction instead of owning our decisions.

When we truly understand this concept—that our lives are shaped by the choices we make—it can be a game-changer. It means that if we're unhappy, it's because we've chosen to be, whether we realise it or not. Life will always present challenges; it will always throw obstacles in our path. Just because something is difficult however, doesn't mean it's impossible. Some things may take longer to achieve, but that doesn't mean they're out of reach.

So, the next time you find yourself complaining about your life, I invite you to pause and ask yourself a powerful question: What am I doing to contribute to this unhappiness? What choices am I making that are keeping me stuck? Most importantly of all, what can I do differently?

The answers may not be easy. They may require courage, effort and a willingness to step into the unknown. If everything in life is a choice though, then it's within your power to choose differently.

You are the only one holding yourself back.

Key Takeaways

1. **Happiness is a Choice, Not Just a Circumstance:** Your level of happiness isn't solely dictated by external circumstances. It's shaped by the choices you make every day. Recognise that you have more control over your happiness than you might think.
2. **Fear of Change Can Keep You Stuck:** Often we avoid making changes because we're scared of the unknown. This fear can lead to self-sabotage, keeping us within our comfort zones even when those zones aren't where we truly want to be.
3. **Personal Responsibility is Empowering:** Understanding that you are responsible for your own life—your happiness, your progress, your relationships—can be incredibly empowering. When you stop blaming external factors, you can start making choices that align with the life you want.

Actionable Tips

- **Start Small and Build Momentum.** Take one small step towards improving an area of your life where you feel unhappy. It could be as simple as dedicating 10 minutes a day to a new hobby, reaching out to someone you've been meaning to reconnect with or researching ways to advance your career. Small actions build momentum and gradually shift you out of stagnation.

- **Challenge Your Excuses.** The next time you catch yourself making excuses for why you can't do something, pause and challenge that thought. Ask yourself, "Is this really true or is it just a story I'm telling myself to avoid taking action?" Reframe the excuse and think of one thing you *can* do to move forward.

- **Set Intentional Daily Choices.** Every morning, set an intention for how you want to approach your day. Decide on one thing you will do that brings you closer to happiness—whether it's practising gratitude, being more mindful in your interactions or pushing yourself to try something new. These daily choices, no matter how small, add up to significant change over time.

2

The Lifelong Student

As humans, there's a moment in our lives where we feel we've figured it out. We believe we know enough about a situation to navigate it with confidence. This is when our ego often whispers that we've done enough, that we know all we need to know. In this very moment however, is where the real journey begins.

I recently read a fascinating book called *Ego is the Enemy* by Ryan Holiday and it delves deeply into this concept. One quote from the book that resonated with me is the idea of always staying a student—learning from everyone and everything around us. In life, it's all too easy to feel like we've reached our destination. Take moving to a new country, for example. After you've handled all the bureaucracy, settled into a routine and found your rhythm, it might seem like you've done everything you need to do. In reality though, the journey has only just begun.

At the time of writing, I've been living in South Italy for six years and let me tell you, I'm still learning. I've realised that I'll never know everything and that's okay. There's still so much more to explore, to talk about and to share. Even through the content I create, there's always another layer to uncover, another lesson to learn. This awareness keeps me grounded in the idea that I don't have all the answers—and likely never will - but that's the beauty of it.

I've committed myself to being a lifelong learner, always striving to be 1% better, as James Clear talks about in the book, *Atomic Habits*. This commitment keeps my ego in check and prevents me from becoming stagnant. I've seen how ego can freeze people in time, trapping them in a cycle of complacency. When people stop learning, they stop growing. Their lives become stuck and what was once a vibrant existence becomes dull and lifeless.

The principle of learning from everyone and everything is crucial. Everyone is your teacher—the people who love you, the people who irritate you and even the people who challenge you. There's a lesson in every interaction, every situation, whether it's positive or negative. This mindset transforms every experience into an opportunity for growth.

When we achieve something significant, it's easy for our ego to pat us on the back and tell us we've made it. Do we ever truly arrive though? Or is life more like a video game, with multiple levels, each presenting new obstacles, challenges, blessings and opportunities? I believe life is about progressing through these levels, each one teaching us something new, pushing us to grow and evolve.

We don't go through life at the same age forever for a reason. We age, we experience different things and we encounter various challenges at different stages of our lives because we're *meant* to keep learning. We're not supposed to remain the same. The people I'm drawn to, the ones I enjoy spending time with, are those who embody this principle. They are lifelong learners, constantly seeking to improve and grow.

Life is what you make of it. While there are many variables beyond our control, there are also countless things we can influence. Often, the difference lies in our willingness to learn, to do things differently, to step out of our comfort zones. Change and success don't come without effort. They require action, growth and an ever-expanding knowledge base.

Interestingly, I've found that feeling too comfortable in life can become uncomfortable. When you're always comfortable, you're not growing. You're not pushing yourself. You're not learning. When you stop learning, you close yourself off to new perspectives and new ideas. This is where closed-mindedness creeps in, leading to narrow views and limited beliefs.

Embrace being a lifelong student. Learn from everyone and everything around you. When you feel like you've arrived, pause and ask yourself how much of that feeling is driven by your ego. Is it really true? The truth is, we never truly arrive. Life is a journey, with each level offering new lessons and new growth.

Maybe the only time we truly arrive is when our journey on this Earth ends. Until then, we're here to learn, to grow and to continue evolving. Yes, celebrate your achievements, be grateful for your successes, but always keep that hunger to learn more, to do more, to be more because that's what it means to be human.

Keep learning. Keep growing. Keep moving forward. The journey is far from over.

Key Takeaways

1. **Never Stop Being a Student:** Life is an ongoing journey of learning and the moment you feel you've "arrived" is often when you stop growing. Embrace the idea that you are always a student, with something new to learn from every experience and every person you encounter.
2. **Challenge Your Comfort Zone:** Comfort is the enemy of growth. When you find yourself in a routine where everything feels too comfortable, it's a sign that you need to push yourself further. Growth happens when you step outside your comfort zone and embrace new challenges.
3. **Learn from Everyone and Everything:** Every person and situation in your life is a potential teacher. Whether the experience is positive or negative, there's always a lesson to be learnt. This mindset transforms challenges into opportunities for growth.

Actionable Tips

- **Make it a habit to seek out new knowledge daily.** This could be through reading a book, engaging in a meaningful conversation or simply observing the world around you. Start a journal where you reflect on what you've learnt each day, no matter how small.
- **Identify one area of your life where you've become too comfortable.** Set a small, achievable goal that pushes you slightly beyond what feels easy—whether it's learning a new skill, meeting new people or tackling a project you've been avoiding.
- **"What can I learn from this?"** The next time you find yourself in a difficult situation or interacting with someone who frustrates

you, pause and ask yourself, "What can I learn from this?" Write down your reflections and consider how you can apply the lesson to improve yourself or your circumstances.

12

3

Redefining Comparison

Comparison. It's a word that often stirs up mixed emotions, doesn't it?

For many of us, comparison is a daily companion—sometimes a quiet whisper in the background, other times a loud, relentless critic. It's a complex, multifaceted aspect of life that has the power to both inspire and destroy. It's something that I've grappled with intensely, especially since moving to South Italy.

I want to start by saying that comparison, when viewed through the right lens, doesn't have to be the enemy. In fact, it can be a powerful ally, guiding us towards our deepest desires and untapped potential. However this hasn't always been my perspective. For a long time, comparison was a source of immense pain, a raw nerve that led to one of the darkest moments of my life.

I still remember Christmas Eve of 2019 vividly. I was wandering around the streets of Palermo, surrounded by what seemed to be a scene straight out of a holiday film. Couples were walking hand in hand, families were gathered together, festive music filled the air and the Christmas lights twinkled brightly. Everything around me felt perfect. Everything….but me. In that moment, I felt utterly alone, consumed by the belief that I wasn't good enough. It was the final straw that contributed to my breakdown.

Looking back now, with the clarity that only time can provide, I realise how distorted my perspective was. When we're caught in the trap of comparison, it's almost impossible to see things as they truly are. We get lost in a fog where fact and fiction blend together. I didn't see the reality of those couples' relationships—whether they were genuinely happy or merely putting on a show. I didn't know if the shops playing festive tunes were struggling to stay afloat or if the city's Christmas lights were masking its own inadequacies. I only saw what my skewed perspective allowed me to see.

This is the insidious nature of comparison. It can leave us with a distorted view of life, one that's far removed from reality. Social media and society, in general, don't make this any easier. Just a quick scroll through Instagram or TikTok is enough to make anyone feel inadequate. What we often forget though, is that we're all imperfect. Every person, every situation, has its flaws. When we compare ourselves to others, we're comparing our messy, imperfect reality to a curated, often idealised version of someone else's life.

This truth hits even harder when you're living as an expat, like I am. Being in a foreign country, away from familiar surroundings, amplifies the urge to compare. For me, family has been a significant source of comparison. Italian families, as I've come to know, are typically close-knit, often seeing each other regularly. My own family, on the other hand, is scattered across the globe and we're not as close as we could be. It's easy to romanticise the Italian family dynamic and feel like something is lacking in my own but the reality is, not every Italian family is perfect. Many have their own set of problems and struggles. It's important to take off the rose-tinted glasses and see things for what they really are.

This romanticised view isn't just limited to families. I see it often on my YouTube channel. People have this idealised vision of life in Italy and I'm passionate about showing them the reality, warts and all. There are plenty of beautiful aspects to life here, but it's not all sunshine and roses. Whenever I post a video that reveals the raw, unfiltered truth, I often get mixed reactions. For every person who appreciates my honesty, there's another who feels disappointed, even upset, that their illusion of Italy has been shattered. This again, is where comparison comes into play. We tend to see things as we want to see them, not as they really are.

I remember when I first moved to South Italy, I was struck by how every Italian woman seemed to have a designer handbag. My initial thought was, "Wow, people here must have money to spend!" It was only later that I discovered how widespread counterfeit goods are here and that many of those bags were far from genuine. It's funny how we let ourselves form judgments based on incomplete information, often influenced by comparison.

Here's where the shift happens though. Comparison doesn't have to be a negative force in our lives. If we can redefine it, we can use it as a tool for growth. I've come to see comparison not as something that diminishes me, but as a guide. It's often a reflection of something within us that's unfulfilled, a desire or a dream that hasn't yet been realised.

When I feel that pang of comparison, I try to see it as a signpost, pointing me towards something I want to achieve.

For instance, in the world of content creation, it's easy to get caught up in what others are doing. I see other YouTube channels with hundreds of thousands of subscribers and videos with millions of views and it's tempting to let that make me feel small, like I'll never measure up. Instead of letting that comparison paralyse me, I've started using it as a guide. It's a reminder of where I want to go, but I've learnt not to let it distract me from my own path. I focus on what I have, what I'm building and the community I'm growing on my channel. It's about honing in on my unique voice and staying true to the content that resonates with my audience.

Redefining comparison is about shifting our focus. It's not about what others have or what they're doing. It's about looking inward and recognising what we truly desire. When we feel that pull of comparison, it's an opportunity to reflect on what's missing in our own lives and how we can take steps towards achieving it. It's about using comparison as a catalyst for growth, rather than a source of self-doubt.

So, the next time you find yourself comparing your life to someone else's, take a step back. Ask yourself what that comparison is really telling you. Is it pointing to something you want to change or achieve? Use it as a guide, a roadmap to your desires and let it lead you towards a more fulfilled, authentic life.

Remember, no one's life is perfect. We're all navigating our own struggles and challenges, even if they're not always visible. So, let's redefine comparison together and turn it into something that empowers us, rather than holds us back.

Key Takeaways

1. **Comparison Distorts Reality:** When we compare ourselves to others, especially through the lens of social media or societal expectations, we often end up with a skewed perspective. It's easy to see only the highlights of others' lives and overlook the full picture. Recognise that what you see isn't always the complete story.

2. **Comparison as a Guide, Not a Judge:** Instead of letting comparison make you feel inadequate, use it as a tool to understand your own desires and goals. Comparison can highlight areas of your life that you want to improve, serving as a guide to help you move in the right direction.

3. **Focus on Your Own Journey:** Everyone's path is unique and what works for someone else may not be right for you. Stay focused on your own progress and measure your success by your own standards, not by what others are doing.

Actionable Tips

- **Shift Your Perspective.** The next time you catch yourself comparing your life to someone else's, pause and reflect. Ask yourself if you're seeing the full picture or just a carefully curated version. Remind yourself that everyone has struggles, even if they aren't visible.

- **Turn Comparison into Motivation.** When you feel the pull of comparison, use it as a moment of self-reflection. What is it that you admire in someone else's life? How can you incorporate those qualities or achievements into your own life in a way that's authentic to you?

- **Create a Vision Board for Your Goals.** Instead of focusing on what others have, create a vision board that reflects your own dreams and aspirations. Fill it with images, quotes and goals that inspire you. Let it be a constant reminder of where you're heading and what truly matters to you, independent of what others are doing.

4

Navigating the Heart vs. Head Crossroads

When we find ourselves at a crossroads, life often presents a classic tug-of-war between the heart and the head.

The challenge is that the heart and the head often speak different languages. The heart is all about passion and dreams, while the head is grounded in practicality and caution. Balancing these forces can be daunting, but it's essential for making a decision that you'll look back on without regret.

Let me take you back a few years to a pivotal moment in my life. I was once a Police Officer in one of the busiest boroughs in London, a role that seemed secure and promising. My career as a Metropolitan Police Officer felt like it was one I would follow for the remainder of my working life. There were rigorous exams, intense training and a sense of duty that I had embraced wholeheartedly.

Yet, despite the perceived safety of this path, something inside me stirred with the desire for a new challenge. I decided to leave behind the certainty of a Police career and venture into the unknown world of entrepreneurship. It wasn't a decision driven by a clear-cut plan or extensive experience but rather by a raw, fearless impulse to follow a new dream.

Starting a business from scratch was an act of courage and self-belief. I had to learn the ropes of running a business on my own, without a mentor or a guide. The risk was significant, but the payoff was worth every challenge. This leap of faith taught me invaluable life skills and showed me that sometimes, the heart's audacious desires lead us to the most fulfilling destinations.

Fast forward to my current life in Italy though and the landscape has changed. Living in a foreign country has introduced a new set of challenges. The bureaucracy here is complex and the language barrier sometimes feels like a brick wall. I find myself more cautious now, unsure if it's age or the unfamiliar environment that has made me more hesitant to take risks.

In my home country, I was used to a certain level of support and understanding in pursuing my dreams. Here in Italy, the culture values security and stability, often prioritising them over passion. This cultural difference has made me reflect deeply on my decisions. I've learnt that when you're in an unfamiliar environment, even small risks can seem monumental.

The essence of being at a crossroads lies in how you balance your heart and head. The heart, with its dreams and passions, urges you to follow what you love. It's the part of you that envisions a life full of fulfilment and joy. The head, on the other hand, is practical, concerned with safety and the potential pitfalls.

When making a significant decision, it's crucial to listen more closely to your heart. Ignoring your inner desires often leads to regret. I've seen many people reflect on their lives with a sense of "what if" rather than "I tried." The latter, even if it leads to failure, is far better than a life filled with missed opportunities.

Cultural influences can also play a significant role in how we approach life's crossroads. In Italy, for instance, there is a strong preference for job security. Many people aspire for an "indeterminato" work contract, a position with no fixed end date, even if it means accepting less than ideal conditions. This cultural norm emphasises security over passion and can make stepping outside of conventional paths feel intimidating.

However, consider this: if you find yourself settling for less than you deserve or sacrificing your passions for the sake of stability, what does that say about how you value yourself? It's essential to assess whether you are choosing comfort over growth and if that decision will ultimately bring you contentment or regret.

As you stand at your own crossroads, I encourage you to trust in your journey. It might not unfold as you planned and it may come with discomfort and challenges. However in the grand scheme of things, it's far more rewarding to pursue what truly makes you happy, even if it means stepping into the unknown.

Remember, it's not about avoiding failure but about embracing the journey with all its uncertainties. Listen to your heart, weigh the practical aspects with your head and move forward with confidence. At the end of the day, living a life true to yourself will be the greatest achievement of all.

Key Takeaways

1. **Balance Passion with Practicality**: At a crossroads, you'll often find yourself torn between following your heart's dreams and your head's practical concerns. Both aspects are crucial in decision-making, but finding a balance can lead to a more fulfilling path.
2. **Embrace the Unfamiliar and Be Brave:** Moving out of your comfort zone, whether by living in a new country or shifting careers, can make risks seem more daunting. However, stepping into the unknown often leads to growth and new opportunities.
3. **Reflect on Your Future Self:** When making significant decisions, it helps to consider how you will view your choices in the future. Will you look back with pride or regret? This perspective can guide you toward decisions that align with your deeper desires.

Actionable Tips

- **Create a list of your passions and dreams alongside a list of practical considerations and potential risks.** Reflect on how each option aligns with your long-term goals and values. Aim to integrate your passions into a practical plan rather than choosing one over the other. For example, if you want to start a business, outline a phased approach that mitigates risks while allowing you to pursue your passion.
- **Break things down**. If you're in a foreign environment or facing a new challenge, break down your fears into smaller, manageable steps. For instance, if you're in a new country and find bureaucracy overwhelming, tackle one administrative task at a time. This approach makes the process less intimidating and helps build

confidence. Remember, bravery isn't the absence of fear but the willingness to face it.

- **Future You.** Imagine yourself at the end of your life, looking back on this moment. Write a letter to your future self detailing what you hope to achieve and how you wish to feel about the decisions you make today. This exercise can provide clarity and motivate you to take actions that align with your long-term vision. Use this reflection to guide your choices, ensuring they contribute to a fulfilling and regret-free life.

5

The Art of Boundaries

There's a concept in life, that's both profoundly simple and incredibly complex—boundaries. I've spent years grappling with the need for boundaries, especially here in South Italy, where the concept seems as elusive as a summer breeze.

So, what's all the fuss about boundaries? In essence, they're the invisible lines you draw to protect your physical, mental and emotional wellbeing. They help you create a balanced life, ensuring that no single aspect-be it work, social life or personal hobbies-takes over. Without these boundaries, you're likely to find yourself in a perpetual state of imbalance, constantly juggling demands and expectations.

Boundaries aren't about being rigid or unkind. Instead, they're about setting limits to safeguard your health and happiness. Saying no can be tough, particularly if you're a people pleaser who wants to make everyone happy. Remember though, having boundaries means saying no respectfully and firmly, without apologising for taking care of yourself. It's a tough lesson I've learnt the hard way and it's something

I hope to pass on to you.

Living in South Italy has given me a unique perspective on boundaries. Here, it seems that boundaries are more of a suggestion than a rule. People often accept things they shouldn't and tolerate behaviours that would make many elsewhere cringe. This cultural norm can make it even more challenging to establish and maintain your own boundaries.

From my experience, the Italian mindset often glorifies enduring discomfort for the sake of keeping a job or avoiding conflict. While there's something admirable about resilience, it's crucial to recognise that this approach can be detrimental to your wellbeing. Boundaries aren't just personal preferences—they're essential for a healthy and fulfilling life.

Let's talk about how boundaries can manifest in your day-to-day life. For instance, setting limits on your technology use can make a huge difference. Decide on a cut-off time for checking emails or social media and stick to it. Create space for face-to-face interactions with loved ones without the constant buzz of notifications. This simple act of disconnecting can refresh your mind and strengthen your relationships.

Another area where boundaries are crucial is in pursuing your passions. I know how easy it is to get lost in a hobby or work project, especially when you're passionate about it. However it's essential to carve out time for other activities and relationships. Balance is key, and establishing boundaries around your time ensures that you don't end up burning out or neglecting other important aspects of your life.

Implementing boundaries can sometimes upset others, especially those who don't have any of their own. It's a strange dynamic—people might perceive your boundaries as a personal affront. However, it's important to remember that their reactions are more about their discomfort with their own lack of boundaries than about you.

Setting boundaries is about being true to yourself and respecting your own limits. It's not about making everyone happy or avoiding conflict. When you start to set boundaries, you might encounter resistance, but it's crucial to stand firm. Your well-being is worth any discomfort that might come from others.

Here's a tip to help you navigate boundaries: ask yourself if a task or activity brings you joy. Marie Kondo, the Queen of decluttering, talks about items sparking joy. Apply the same principle to your tasks and commitments. If something feels burdensome or overwhelming, it might be time to reassess your boundaries.

The next time you're faced with a decision, think about whether it aligns with your boundaries and brings you joy. It's a small but powerful step towards a more balanced and fulfilling life.

Key Takeaways

1. **Embrace the Power of "No":** Boundaries are essential for maintaining balance and protecting your wellbeing. They help you set limits and ensure that you don't end up overwhelmed or burnt out.
2. **Be Aware of Cultural and Personal Differences:** Boundaries can be challenging to establish, especially in environments where they're not commonly practised or appreciated. This is especially true in cultures where enduring discomfort is normalised, so

having an awareness of this can help

3. **Find Joy in Your Boundaries:** Boundaries help you manage your time and energy, ensuring you focus on what truly brings you joy and prevents burnout.

Actionable Tips

- **Practice saying "no" without guilt.** Start small by turning down minor requests or commitments that don't align with your priorities. Remember, "No" is a complete sentence. You don't owe anyone a lengthy explanation or justification.
- **Reflect on the cultural norms around you.** How do they influence your personal boundaries? Identify areas where you can start asserting your boundaries gently but firmly and remain consistent despite potential pushback.
- **Regularly evaluate your activities and commitments.** Ask yourself if each task or engagement adds value to your life. If it doesn't spark joy or align with your values, consider setting boundaries to protect your time and energy.

6

The Books That Have Changed My Perspective

It's strange to think of reading as a forgotten art form, but up until recently, that's exactly what it had become in my life. As a child, I was a voracious reader, devouring books with the same enthusiasm that you might devour a bar of chocolate. My parent's home was filled with books, each one offering a new adventure, a new world to explore. However as I grew older and technology began to dominate my life, my love for reading gradually faded. I found myself more often scrolling through social media than losing myself in a good book.

Then, a few years ago, something shifted. One summer in Italy, the realisation hit me—I had barely read a single book that year. This was a painful truth to face and it made me deeply sad. So, I made a commitment to myself. Every morning, I would spend at least 15 minutes reading. It was a small change, but it had a profound impact. In 2023, this habit led me to some truly incredible books that didn't just entertain me—they changed my life.

Reading is underrated, but it has the power to transform your perspective, expand your mind and take you to places you've never imagined. I hope that by sharing these books with you, I can inspire you to pick up a book, invest in yourself and (re)discover the transformative power of reading.

The Seven Habits of Highly Effective People by Stephen Covey

The first book that made a significant impact on me was Stephen Covey's classic, *The Seven Habits of Highly Effective People*. I had heard about this book for years, but it wasn't until the beginning of 2023, that I felt it was my time to read it. Books, I believe, choose you when the moment is right and this one couldn't have chosen a better time.

Covey's book is divided into seven habits, each one a principle that guides you towards personal and professional effectiveness:

1. **Be Proactive:** You are in charge of your life.
2. **Begin with the End in Mind:** Always have a plan.
3. **Put First Things First:** Work first, then play.
4. **Think Win-Win:** Everyone can win.
5. **Seek First to Understand, Then to Be Understood:** Listen before you speak.
6. **Synergise:** Together is better.
7. **Sharpen the Saw:** Balance is best.

This book reminded me of something essential—we are responsible for our own lives. It's easy to blame external circumstances for where we are, but in doing so, we strip away our power. We allow ourselves to become weak, dependent on others for our happiness and success.

Covey's message is clear: we are responsible for our choices and we have the power to shape our own lives.

One quote that particularly resonated with me was, "Let negative energy fly out open windows. Don't take it in." It's a simple yet profound reminder that while we can't control the negativity around us, we can choose not to let it affect us. We don't have to absorb other people's negativity. Instead, we can let it fly out the window and focus on protecting our own energy.

Another powerful quote from Covey's book is, "Investment in ourselves is the single most powerful investment we can ever make in our lives." This idea ties in with the habit of sharpening the saw—taking the time to invest in our own growth and well-being. Whether it's through education, developing new skills or simply taking better care of our health, the investment we make in ourselves pays the greatest dividends.

Create Something Awesome by Roberto Blake

The next book that had a profound effect on me was *Create Something Awesome* by Roberto Blake. Blake is a well-known YouTuber and content creator who shares his wisdom on how to profit from your passion. Even if you're not a content creator, the lessons in this book are invaluable.

One quote that stood out to me was, "Anyone who doesn't invest in their dreams can't be surprised by the lack of them." This echoes Covey's ideas about the importance of investing in ourselves. Whether it's financial investment or the investment of time, if we don't put in the effort, we can't expect our dreams to come true. This is a beautiful reminder that we have to make time for the things that matter to us.

Another quote that really hit home was, "Being above average is a choice." It's easy to look at successful people and attribute their success to luck or circumstance, but more often than not, their success is the result of hard work and dedication. Choosing to be above average means choosing to put in the effort, to make the sacrifices and to take the necessary steps towards your goals.

The Art and Business of Online Writing by Nicolas Cole

As someone who spends a lot of time online, Nicolas Cole's *The Art and Business of Online Writing* was a game-changer for me. This book is essentially a manual for how to write effectively in the online world, where attention spans are shorter and competition for that attention is fierce.

One of the most impactful quotes from this book is, "The number of hours I spend consuming should never equal or exceed the number of hours I spend creating." In today's world, it's easy to get caught up in what others are doing, to spend hours consuming content rather than creating it. This quote reminded me that while it's important to stay informed, our primary focus should always be on creation.

Another insightful quote from Cole's book is, "You are not the main character in your story, your reader is." This is a harsh truth, but an important one. When we create content, especially online, it's easy to fall into the trap of making it all about us. However if we want to truly connect with our audience, we have to put them first. We have to create content that serves them, not just ourselves.

The Psychology of Money by Morgan Housel

Morgan Housel's *The Psychology of Money* was another standout read. This book delves into the complex relationship we have with money and how our behaviour around it can shape our lives.

One quote that really struck me was, "Luck and risk are cousins." This is such a powerful reminder that taking risks is an essential part of life. Every risk carries the potential for both success and failure, but without taking those risks, we'll never have the opportunity to succeed. I've taken many risks in my life—from leaving a stable job to starting a business, to moving to a new country—and each one has taught me invaluable lessons.

Another quote from Housel's book that resonated with me is, "Controlling our time is the highest dividend money pays." We often think of money in terms of what it can buy, but its true value lies in the freedom it can provide. Money can buy us time—time to do the things we love, to spend with the people we care about and to live life on our own terms.

Make Time by Jake Knapp and John Zeratsky

Finally, *Make Time* by Jake Knapp and John Zeratsky offered practical advice on how to focus on what really matters each day. One concept that stood out to me was the idea of how we divide our time into two categories: the "busy bandwagons" and the "infinity pools." The busy bandwagons are the endless to-do lists that keep us constantly occupied, while the infinity pools are the never-ending distractions of social media and technology.

Another powerful takeaway was the idea of having a "personal sprint"—dedicating five days to focus on one project. This concept is a game-changer for anyone with a passion project or a goal they're struggling to achieve. By focusing all of your energy on one thing for a short, intense period, you can make significant progress and avoid the trap of spreading yourself too thin.

Key Takeaways

1. **You Are in Control of Your Life.** One of the most powerful lessons from *The Seven Habits of Highly Effective People* is that you are responsible for your own life. It's easy to blame circumstances, other people, or bad luck for where you are, but at the end of the day, your choices shape your reality.
2. **Invest in Yourself.** Both Stephen Covey and Roberto Blake emphasise the importance of investing in yourself. Whether through education, skill development, or self-care, the returns on these investments are immeasurable.
3. **Prioritise Creation Over Consumption**. In a world full of distractions, it's easy to spend more time consuming content than creating it. However, the true value comes from what you create, not what you consume.

Actionable Tips

- **Start each day with a proactive mindset.** Before you dive into your tasks, take five minutes to set clear intentions. Identify one area where you can take more control—whether it's your health, your career or your relationships—and commit to making one small, positive change. It could be as simple as choosing to respond calmly in a stressful situation or dedicating time to a personal goal.

- **Make personal development a daily habit**. Start by setting aside 15 minutes each day for self-improvement—read a book, take an online course or practise a new skill. Treat this time as non-negotiable, just like you would a meeting or an appointment. Over time, these small investments will compound, leading to significant growth.
- **Set a daily creation goal.** Whether it's writing a blog post, designing a graphic or working on a project, aim to create something every day. To balance your time, try this simple rule: for every thirty minutes you spend consuming content, spend at least an hour creating. This will shift your focus from passive consumption to active creation, helping you make meaningful progress toward your goals.

7

Rethinking Your Year: The Power of 12 Weeks

At the dawn of every New Year, you probably notice how social media is suddenly awash with reflections on the past year and optimism for the one ahead. This ritual of looking back and setting new goals is something we all participate in, to some extent. Here's the thing: What if our lives could look radically different if we didn't wait for January to roll around before becoming intentional with our reflections and objectives? What if we rethought how we approached our year entirely?

This is where the concept of, *The 12 Week Year,* comes in—a book by Brian Moran and Michael Lennington that has fundamentally changed how I view goal setting. The idea is simple yet powerful: instead of seeing your year as 12 months, break it down into four 12-week segments. Essentially, you're compressing your year into shorter, more intense periods of focus and productivity. By the end of a traditional 12-month year, you could have accomplished the equivalent of four years of progress.

Now, why does this work so well? For starters, when you're setting goals for just three months at a time, you're more likely to achieve them. Why? Simply because you're interested and engaged in what you're pursuing during that specific period of your life. Think about it—how often have you set goals in January, only to find that by June or July, your interests and priorities have shifted? It's human nature to change, to evolve and sometimes, what seemed important in January no longer resonates with you halfway through the year.

With this 12-week system though, your goals remain fresh, relevant and most importantly, achievable. You're not staring at a daunting 12-month timeline, wondering how you're going to stay motivated for such a long stretch. Instead, you have a clear, immediate focus. It's much easier to stay committed to a goal when you know you'll be re-evaluating and setting new ones in just a few weeks. This creates a sense of urgency that drives you to take action.

Another reason this method is so effective is that it aligns with how we naturally work. Think about how your activities tend to expand to fill the time you have available. If you give yourself an entire year to achieve something, chances are you'll take the entire year—or worse, lose interest and abandon it altogether. However if you set a goal for three months, your focus sharpens and you're much more likely to push through and achieve it because the time frame is short and the end is in sight.

I experienced the power of this approach first-hand at the beginning of 2023. In the first three months, I accomplished things that would have taken me much longer had I approached them with a traditional yearly mindset. I created a set of merchandise from scratch, sourced an online shop provider, designed and marketed my shop and launched it—all within about a month and a half. I also stuck to a daily Italian study regime for the entire three months. These are the kinds of achievements that can feel daunting over a longer period but become manageable and even exciting within a 12-week time frame.

What I found most remarkable was how much more I accomplished in those three months compared to previous years when I had set goals for the entire year. This method isn't just about getting more done; it's about staying engaged and motivated because your goals are always fresh and relevant to where you are in life at that moment.

The best part of it all is that the excitement and anticipation we all feel in January as we look forward to the New Year, you can experience every 12 weeks. Imagine the momentum you could build if, every three months, you had that same sense of renewal, that same drive to reflect, set new goals and move forward with purpose. Instead of forgetting the small but significant moments throughout the year, you'll be more attuned to them, tracking your progress weekly, capturing lessons learnt and carrying those insights into your next 12-week cycle.

I understand that goal setting isn't for everyone. In fact, living in South Italy, I've noticed that people here don't seem as invested in this practice as those in other parts of the world, like the UK. Many people I speak to either don't know what their objectives are for the year or simply aren't interested in setting any. There's a strong culture of living in the present moment, which is beautiful in its own right. However whilst living in the present is valuable, it's also important to acknowledge that some experiences and growth require planning, goals and a sense of direction.

When I look back at my own life, the things I've achieved wouldn't have been possible without setting goals. Even before I adopted the 12-week year approach, traditional goal setting gave me something to focus on, something to strive for. Without it, I would have drifted through life with no real purpose, and that, to me, is like a living hell. Having a purpose, a focus and something that propels you forward is how you truly experience the richness of life.

So, as you think about your own journey, I encourage you to experiment with the 12-week year method. Whether you're in a culture where goal setting is a big deal or not, give it a try and see what you can achieve. You might find that this approach not only inspires positive change in your life but also brings a sense of excitement and purpose to your year that you've never experienced before.

Key Takeaways

1. **Break the Year into Manageable Chunks**: Instead of viewing the year as a daunting 12-month stretch, see it as four distinct 12-week periods. This makes goal setting more manageable and keeps your focus sharp and immediate.
2. **Leverage the Power of Urgency**: Shorter time frames naturally create a sense of urgency. You're more likely to stay committed to goals that feel pressing and relevant, rather than ones that seem distant and easy to put off.
3. **Capture and Reflect on Progress Regularly**: By breaking the year into 12-week cycles, you give yourself more opportunities to reflect, adjust, and celebrate small wins. This keeps you engaged and helps you remember the little moments that often get lost in a traditional yearly review.

Actionable Tips

- **Set 12-Week Goals Today**: Don't wait until January to set your goals. Start by identifying what you want to achieve in the next 12 weeks. Write down three to five key objectives that are meaningful and achievable within this time frame.
- **Create a Weekly Reflection Practice**. Every week, set aside time to reflect on your progress. Ask yourself what's working, what's not and what adjustments you need to make. This will keep your goals top of mind and help you stay on track.
- **Celebrate Every 12 Weeks**. At the end of each 12-week period, take time to celebrate your achievements, no matter how small. Reflect on the lessons you've learnt and use them to fuel your enthusiasm for the next 12-week cycle. This will help maintain your momentum and keep you excited about your journey.

8

Embracing the 12-Week Year - My Case Study

One of my goals for my first 12 weeks was to develop a consistent Italian study routine. Now, if you've ever tried to learn a new language, you know it can be a bit of a roller coaster. I've been living in Italy for six years and while I've always recognised the importance of mastering the language, my progress has been inconsistent.

This time though, I approached it with a renewed strategy. I set a simple, manageable goal: study Italian daily. It didn't matter if I could only spare 15 minutes on some days; the key was consistency. This wasn't about cramming or overwhelming myself with too many tasks. By focusing on just one goal and integrating it into my daily routine, I developed a habit that has become a part of my life. I now miss it when I don't study and that's a milestone I'm truly proud of.

Another goal was to enhance my YouTube presence. As anyone who's ventured into the world of YouTube knows, it's not a quick-fix platform. Growth comes with consistent effort and patience. In the past, my posting schedule was erratic—sometimes weekly, sometimes not at all. This inconsistency stalled my channel's growth.

By embracing the 12-Week Year, I committed to a rigorous posting schedule: two long-form videos, three shorts, and two Community posts each week. The results? Phenomenal. My channel's performance soared by 200% compared to the previous year. I even beat the predictions from Social Blade, a site that is often recognised for its accuracy in predicting the growth of social channels. This surge in engagement was a direct result of focusing on consistency and adapting to what worked best for my audience.

One of the most enlightening aspects of the 12-Week Year is its flexibility. While I had planned to design digital products, I faced unexpected resistance. I realised that this wasn't something I was truly passionate about at the moment. Instead of sticking rigidly to this goal, I reassessed and pivoted towards offering services, which felt much more aligned with my interests and strengths.

This flexibility is one of the system's greatest strengths. You're not locked into a rigid plan; rather, you're encouraged to evaluate and adjust your goals based on what's working and what's not. It's a dynamic process that keeps you agile and responsive to your evolving needs and desires.

As I wrapped up my first 12-week cycle, I took time to reflect and celebrate my achievements. It's so easy to rush from one goal to the next without pausing to acknowledge your progress. Celebrating your successes, no matter how small, is crucial. It's not just about marking a finish line; it's about recognising your efforts and enjoying the journey. As you complete each 12-week year, take a moment to reflect on what you've accomplished. Use this time to recharge and set new, exciting goals for the upcoming cycle.

Even if you're starting mid-way through the year, it's never too late to adopt the 12-Week Year principle. The beauty of this approach is that it's flexible and adaptable. Whether you're looking to master a new skill, grow your business, or simply make the most of your time, this method can help you achieve more than you ever thought possible.

Remember, the way you use your time can make all the difference. By breaking your year into manageable, focused periods, you're setting yourself up for success. So take the plunge, set your goals and dive into your next 12 weeks with renewed vigour. You might just surprise yourself with what you can achieve.

Key Takeaways

1. **Embrace the Power of the 12-Week Year.** Viewing your year in 12-week increments rather than 12 months creates a sense of urgency and focus that accelerates progress and boosts productivity.
2. **Prioritise Consistency Over Perfection.** Consistent, daily effort towards your goals yields better results than sporadic bursts of activity. Whether it's studying a new language or growing a social media presence, small, steady actions add up over time.
3. **Stay Flexible and Adapt Your Goals.** The 12-Week Year isn't about rigidly sticking to one plan. It's about evaluating what's working, adapting and making changes as needed to stay aligned with your true priorities and interests.

Actionable Tips

- **Start by mapping out your goals for the next 12 weeks.** Break them into manageable tasks and set weekly milestones to keep yourself on track. Use a planner or digital tool to visualise your plan and regularly check in on your progress. Remember, the shorter time frame helps maintain momentum and prevents procrastination.

- **Identify a key area where you want to build a habit or improve.** Set aside a specific time each day for this activity, even if it's just 15 minutes. For example, if learning a new skill, dedicate a set time each day to practise. If working on social media, establish a posting schedule and stick to it as closely as possible.

- **Regularly review your progress at the end of each week.** Reflect on what's working well and what isn't. If you encounter resistance or find that a particular goal no longer resonates with you, then pivot. Adjust your goals or methods to better align with your current needs and passions. This adaptability ensures you're always moving towards what truly motivates you.

9

Forget Other People

This chapter is all about one thing: forgetting other people.

Yes, you read that right.

It's time to stop looking around for approval, validation or advice from others who, quite frankly, have no clue what your journey is about. Instead, it's time to listen to yourself, trust your instincts and let your inner voice guide you. Let me tell you, that voice inside you knows exactly what you need—better than anyone else ever could.

Here's the reality: other people are not you. That's the first thing we need to remember. We often turn to others for validation, hoping they'll pat us on the back and tell us we're on the right track. How can we expect that though, when they don't share our background, beliefs or even our mindset? The truth is, nobody else is qualified to tell you what's right for *your* life.

Think about it. How many times have you held back on a dream because someone else didn't see it the way you did? How many times have you sought advice only to walk away more confused than ever? That's because we're looking for something in others that they simply can't provide—a conviction that can only come from within.

I've seen it happen too many times. We look to others to give us confidence, to validate our decisions, but that rarely works out. More often than not, their advice is clouded by their own fears, experiences and biases—none of which have anything to do with you or your dreams.

Back when I lived in the UK, I made a bold decision to leave my job in the Police and start my own business. I was excited, confident and felt ready to take on the world. When I told my neighbour though, the first thing she asked was, "How are you going to pay your bills?". No "Congratulations," no "That's amazing!", just a big, fat question mark on my ability to succeed.

Now, you might think that's a fair question, but here's how I took it: as a sign that this person wasn't right to share my dreams with. Her response was coloured by her own fears and limiting beliefs about money, security and probably a lifetime of playing it safe. If I had let that doubt creep in—if I had listened to her instead of myself—I might have retracted my resignation, stuck with the status quo and never built the successful business I ended up creating.

This is what happens when we let other people's fears and limitations influence our decisions. We risk losing sight of our goals and worse, we might never reach the heights we're capable of.

Another aspect is the influence of cultural mindsets, especially if you're living in a different country, like I am. When you live abroad, you'll find that traditional beliefs and deep-rooted cultural values can weigh heavily on your decisions. Take the working culture, for instance. In the South of Italy, where I live, many people treat work like it's family. There's this idea that your workplace is your family and you owe them a level of loyalty that goes beyond the professional sense.

Let me tell you something though: work is not family. Sure, you might have a sense of community and yes, some people might even work with their blood relatives. Family though? No. At the end of the day, if you can be fired from a job, it's not family. Believing otherwise can keep you stuck in situations that don't serve your growth or happiness.

If you buy into these cultural mindsets without questioning them, you might never break free to pursue your own path. That's why it's so crucial to listen to yourself, especially when your goals don't align with the traditional or cultural expectations around you.

So, what's the takeaway here? It's simple: forget other people. Not completely, of course. There's always value in learning from those who've walked the path before you. Success leaves clues after all. However when it comes to your dreams, your goals and your decisions, the most important voice you can listen to is your own.

When you tune out the noise and focus on your own instincts, you minimise the risk of getting derailed by doubt, negativity or fear. You stay true to what you know, deep down, is right for you. Trust me, your inner self always knows. It's just that we get so distracted by the external noise that we forget to listen.

Make it a point to prioritise your own voice. Trust yourself more. At the end of the day, you're the only one who really knows what's best for you.

Key Takeaways

1. **Other People Aren't You:** No one else shares your background, beliefs or mindset. Their advice is often coloured by their own experiences, which may not apply to your unique path.
2. **Trust Your Inner Voice**: Your inner self always knows what's best for you. The more you listen to yourself, the clearer your path will become.
3. **Cultural and Traditional Mindsets Can Hold You Back**. Be aware of how deeply rooted cultural beliefs might influence your decisions. Challenge them if they don't align with your personal goals.

Actionable Tips

- **Practice Self-Reflection**. Start each week with a quiet moment to tune into your inner voice. Ask yourself what you truly want and need, free from external influences.
- **Create Boundaries**. Identify people whose advice often leaves you feeling doubtful or confused. Limit how much you share with them about your dreams and goals.
- **Surround Yourself with Like-Minded Individuals**. Seek out communities or mentors who have walked a similar path and can offer insights that resonate with your journey. Their advice is more likely to be relevant and empowering.

10

Words are Wands

Words are not just mere tools for communication; they are the architects of our reality. Whether we're aware of it or not, the language we use shapes our experiences, influences our emotions and moulds our actions. Words are quite literally like the wands of a wizard or magician.

Imagine your words as seeds you plant in the garden of your life. Just like seeds can grow into beautiful flowers or pesky weeds, the words you use can cultivate a thriving mindset or foster limiting beliefs. I've learnt this first-hand through my journey of learning Italian while living in Italy for six years. Early on, I constantly told myself, "Learning Italian is so difficult," "I'm not good at languages" and "I'm never going to master this." These statements became a self-fulfilling prophecy. Instead of focusing on the progress I was making, I fixated on the challenges, which only ended up reinforcing the difficulties.

Then a shift happened. I decided to transform my approach. Instead of dreading the language learning process, I began to frame it positively. Now, I tell myself, "Learning Italian is interesting," "It's going to be fun" and "This is a challenge I can overcome." By changing my internal dialogue, I've noticed a significant improvement in my motivation and progress. I've already made studying Italian a daily ritual and it feels energising rather than burdensome.

This change in perspective isn't limited to language learning. It's a powerful reminder that our everyday language can either uplift us or bring us down. Consider the way we talk about our jobs, our relationships or even our personal challenges. Frequently, we might say, "I have to go to work," which carries a sense of obligation and resentment. What if we changed that to, "I choose to go to work" or "I get to go to work"? This simple shift in wording can transform how we view our circumstances and enhance our overall satisfaction.

There's the famous expression - If you say you can or you can't, you're always right. This simple sentence highlights just how important our language really is.

When it comes to facing criticism or negativity, especially as a content creator or in any public role, it's crucial to handle it with grace. Negative comments can sting, but responding with kindness and love rather than defensiveness not only reflects our inner strength but also keeps our own spirit intact. Remember, the energy we send out into the world often comes back to us. By responding to negativity with compassion, we create a cycle of positive energy.

By becoming more mindful of the words we use and the energy we put out into the world, we not only improve our own lives but also positively influence those around us.

Let's embrace the power of words to build a more fulfilling and empowered life.

Key Takeaways

1. **Words Shape Reality**: The language we use can either reinforce our limitations or empower our growth. Pay attention to how you speak to yourself and others.
2. **Reframe Your Perspective**: Shifting from negative to positive language can transform your experience and progress, whether it's in learning a new skill or managing daily challenges.
3. **Respond with Kindness**: When faced with negativity or criticism, choose to respond with love and understanding. This not only preserves your peace but also fosters a more positive environment.

Actionable Tips

- **Monitor Your Self-Talk.** Take note of the language you use when talking about yourself or your goals. Replace phrases like "I can't" or "It's too hard" with "I'm learning" or "It's a challenge I'm overcoming."
- **Reframe Obligations.** Change your internal narrative about tasks you find burdensome. Instead of saying "I have to," try saying "I choose to" or "I get to," which can shift your perspective from obligation to opportunity.
- **Respond to Criticism with Compassion.** When faced with negative comments or criticism, practise responding with kindness. Send a positive message back and focus on maintaining your own

high vibe, rather than reacting with negativity.

11

Everything has an Expiry Date

When we think of expiry dates, we usually picture them stamped on milk cartons or fresh produce. What if I told you though, that this idea can extend far beyond the supermarket? Think about the experiences you've had in your life—relationships, jobs, hobbies and even places you've lived. Just like that carton of milk, these experiences also have a shelf life. They can reach a point where they no longer nourish you, where they become stale or even detrimental.

Recently, I was reflecting on my own journey. For four years, I called Salerno, a beautiful city in South Italy, my home. It was a place where I built my life, found myself and created countless memories. Over time though, I began to sense that Salerno had reached its expiry date for me. The city that once filled me with excitement and inspiration had started to feel stagnant. I had lived through its beauty, explored its corners and, honestly, I had hit a wall.

Leaving Salerno wasn't a decision I took lightly. It was where I had settled and where I had built a comfortable life. Sometimes though, comfort can turn into complacency. The fear of change was real. It was tempting to stay in my secure little bubble, but I knew that staying would only lead to resentment and a sense of missed opportunities.

In 2022, I made the decision to move to Palermo. The transition was challenging—Palermo was wild compared to the serenity of Salerno. Yet, this change has been one of the most significant and rewarding decisions of my life. Living in a new city, surrounded by new people and experiences, has sparked incredible growth within me. It's like I was waking up to a fresh perspective, full of new opportunities and inspirations.

Change often comes with fear. We're wired to seek comfort and avoid the unknown. The magic of change lies in its ability to push us beyond our boundaries, to help us grow in ways we never imagined. It's like the difference between a cheese that's gone mouldy and a fresh, exciting new variety. Just as cheese can become unappetizing when past its prime, our lives can become stale if we cling too long to what's no longer serving us.

As we approach a new year or a new phase in life, it's essential to take a moment to evaluate what's working and what's not. Are there aspects of your life that have outlived their usefulness? Are there experiences or situations that no longer bring you joy? Recognising these moments is crucial.

Embracing change is not about abandoning everything you've ever loved or valued. It's about recognising when something has reached its expiry date and being brave enough to make the necessary adjustments. Change doesn't have to be a daunting monster; it can be a beautiful opportunity for growth and enrichment.

When you find yourself in a moment of dissatisfaction or stagnation, ask yourself: What can I do to revitalise my life? How can I step out of my comfort zone to bring new joy and excitement into my experiences?

Change is not just an inevitable part of life—it's a powerful tool for creating a richer, more fulfilling existence. Embrace the expiry dates, make the changes you need and let yourself flourish in new and exciting ways.

Key Takeaways

1. **Life's Experiences Have Expiry Dates**: Just like perishable goods, the experiences and situations in our lives can reach a point where they no longer serve us. Recognizing when this happens is key to avoiding stagnation and resentment.
2. **Change is Essential for Growth**: Embracing change, despite its challenges, is crucial for personal development. It pushes us out of our comfort zones and opens doors to new opportunities and perspectives.
3. **Evaluate and Act**: Regularly assess what aspects of your life bring you joy and fulfillment. If something has become stale, be proactive in making the necessary changes to infuse new energy and excitement into your life.

Actionable Tips

- **Reflect on Your Current Situation**: Take some time to honestly evaluate your life. Identify areas that feel stagnant or uninspiring. Ask yourself if these areas have reached their expiry date and consider how you can address them.
- **Embrace Small Changes**: If the idea of big changes feels overwhelming, start with small adjustments. It could be as simple as exploring a new hobby, meeting new people or altering your daily routine. Small changes can pave the way for bigger transformations.
- **Push Through the Fear**: Acknowledge that fear of change is natural. Instead of letting it hold you back, use it as a motivator to take action. Embrace the discomfort as a sign that you're moving towards growth and new possibilities.

12

Asking the Right Questions

I recently read Steven Bartlett's book - *The Diary of a CEO* - and one quote particularly resonated with me: "Ask questions of your actions and your actions will answer."

It's a powerful reminder that questioning can be more impactful than simply making statements, when it comes to driving change. This idea isn't just a theoretical concept—it's something that I see unfolding in my own life and the lives of those around me.

Living in South Italy, I've witnessed a common pattern: the tendency to blame external factors for local problems. For instance, the ongoing issue of rubbish collection in Palermo has been a seemingly endless source of frustration. Residents often point fingers at the government, the private waste management company or even the broader regional neglect. What I find striking, however, is the disconnect between the words people use to describe their grievances and their actions to address them.

Despite complaints, there's a noticeable lack of personal accountability. People who voice their discontent about overflowing bins and unsightly streets are often the same ones who litter or let their dogs use public spaces as toilets. This contradiction between one's words and actions highlights a broader issue: a lack of self-reflection and responsibility.

This same pattern extends to the workplace. In South Italy, there's a widespread sense of dissatisfaction with working conditions and salaries. Yet, many people accept these conditions without raising their voices or seeking better opportunities. Silence becomes unspoken permission and employers feel no pressure to improve their practices. It's a cycle that perpetuates itself, keeping things exactly as they are.

The critical lesson here is that asking questions can be a powerful tool for change. If individuals and communities start questioning their behaviours and choices, it could spark significant improvements. For instance, asking yourself, "Will I keep the streets as clean as my home?" or "Will I speak up about unfair working conditions?" could lead to tangible changes. It's not about having all the answers right away but about starting the conversation and taking small steps towards improvement.

In a broader context, this principle can be applied to all aspects of life. Whether it's about improving your personal habits, addressing environmental concerns or challenging systemic issues, asking the right questions can guide you towards meaningful action and change.

Asking questions isn't just about finding answers but about prompting action and accountability. It's the first step to transforming your life and making a positive impact on your community.

Key Takeaways

1. **The Power of Questions:** Asking questions about your actions can lead to more effective and meaningful changes than making statements. Questions prompt reflection and responsibility, driving better outcomes.
2. **Disconnect Between Words and Actions:** Observing how people often blame external factors while failing to take personal responsibility highlights a common issue. Addressing this disconnect can lead to improved personal and communal behaviour.
3. **Importance of Speaking Up:** Silence can perpetuate dissatisfaction, particularly in work environments. Voicing concerns and seeking change can drive improvements and encourage others to do the same.

Actionable Tips

- **Practise Self-Questioning.** Regularly ask yourself questions like, "Will I follow through on this goal?" or "Will I take action to improve this situation?". This practice helps you stay accountable and focused on your objectives.
- **Address Contradictions.** If you notice discrepancies between your words and actions, take steps to align them. For example, if you complain about litter but leave rubbish behind, make a conscious effort to dispose of waste properly.
- **Speak Up for Change.** If you're unhappy with your work conditions or other aspects of your life, don't stay silent. Raise your concerns with the appropriate channels and seek solutions. Your voice can initiate change and inspire others to do the same.

13

The Power of 1%

The idea of making a 1% improvement is rooted in the belief that small, consistent actions lead to remarkable results over time. You might have heard this notion echoed in different forms: Steven Bartlett's, *The Diary of a CEO*, talks about it with clarity and James Clear's, *Atomic Habits*, dives into it with scientific backing. Essentially, it's about the magic of incremental gains.

Picture it like this: you're planting a tree. At first, it's just a tiny sapling, barely visible but with daily care—watering, nurturing and a lot of patience—what started as a modest seedling eventually grows into a robust, flourishing tree. The same goes for your personal and professional development. Those small, seemingly insignificant efforts compound, growing into something substantial and impactful.

'Kaizen' is a Japanese term meaning "continuous improvement." This philosophy is more than just a concept; it's a way of life for many. 'Kaizen' teaches us that by focusing on making tiny, consistent improvements, we set ourselves up for greater success and fulfilment.

I find this approach incredibly refreshing. It's about embracing the journey of progress, no matter how minuscule the steps might seem. The beauty of 'Kaizen' is that it aligns perfectly with the 1% principle. It encourages us to see value in the small changes we make every day and to understand that those tiny tweaks are what lead to significant, lasting growth.

For the past six years, I've been living in Italy, immersing myself in the language and culture. Initially, I was overwhelmed by the idea of becoming fluent in the language. It seemed like a monumental task that would require hours of study each day, but here's where the 1% principle came into play.

Instead of trying to cram hours of language study into my busy schedule, I committed to studying Italian for just 15 to 30 minutes each morning. It didn't feel like much, but those short, consistent bursts of practice compounded over time. What seemed like a small effort turned into a significant achievement. The progress I've made over the past month is more substantial than anything I had managed in the previous several months combined. That's the magic of compounding effort.

There's something crucial that we need to address though—our tendency to return to old habits or familiar situations because they feel safe. I've been there myself. I've left jobs, ventured into new territories and then found myself tempted to go back to what was once comfortable. However when we go back, we often find that things have changed. The comfort we once knew is no longer there.

This realisation hit me hard when I returned to a previous job in the UK, only to find that the environment had shifted and the joy I once experienced had vanished. The lesson here is to keep moving forward.

Embrace the philosophy of continuous improvement and avoid falling into the trap of revisiting past situations for the sake of comfort. Life is in constant flux and so should your approach be to growth.

We live in a world obsessed with grand gestures and dramatic successes. We see the highlights of people's achievements and think they must have happened overnight. The truth is, behind every success story are countless small, often overlooked steps. The real work—the blood, sweat and tears—comes from those tiny, consistent efforts.

That's where the 1% principle shines. It's about paying attention to the small stuff, making those incremental changes and understanding that these minor adjustments are what pave the way to achieving big goals. It's not the grand gestures but the steady, persistent actions that lead to lasting success.

Here's the most important part: your commitment to making a 1% improvement each day must come from within. It's easy to rely on external motivation or validation, but true progress happens when you make that commitment to yourself. Your drive should not depend on others; it should be a personal promise to keep moving forward, no matter how small the steps may seem.

Embrace the power of 1%. Commit to making small, daily improvements. It's those seemingly insignificant efforts that, over time, will lead to extraordinary results. Keep going, stay consistent and watch as those small changes accumulate into something truly remarkable.

Key Takeaways

1. **Small Steps Lead to Big Changes:** Embracing the 1% principle means understanding that tiny, consistent improvements can compound over time, leading to significant results. It's not about making grand gestures but about making small, daily efforts that build up to something extraordinary.

2. **The Kaizen Philosophy:** Continuous, incremental improvements are at the heart of 'Kaizen'. This Japanese concept teaches us that the path to greatness is paved with small, steady steps rather than massive, sporadic leaps. By adopting this mindset, you set yourself up for long-term success and personal growth.

3. **Commit to Yourself:** True progress comes from a personal commitment to continuous improvement. External motivation can be fleeting, but your dedication to making a 1% improvement each day should be a promise you make to yourself, regardless of external circumstances or support.

Actionable Tips

- **Start Small and Stay Consistent:**
- Pick a Focus Area. Choose one area in your life or work where you want to improve. It could be learning a new skill, building a healthier habit or enhancing your productivity.
- Set Tiny Goals.Break down your goal into small, manageable tasks. For example, if you want to improve your fitness, start with just 10 minutes of exercise a day. The key is consistency, not intensity.
- **Embrace the 'Kaizen' Approach:**

- Daily Reflection. Spend a few minutes each day reflecting on what small improvements you have made. Celebrate these tiny victories and think about how you can build on them.
- Iterate and Adjust. Regularly review your progress and make minor adjustments to your approach. The goal is to keep evolving and refining your methods to fit your changing needs and circumstances.
- **Commit to the Process:**
- Create a Routine. Establish a daily routine that incorporates your small improvement efforts. Whether it's a morning ritual or an evening review, consistency in your routine reinforces your commitment.
- Track Your Progress. Keep a journal or use an app to track your daily efforts. Seeing your progress over time can be incredibly motivating and helps reinforce the value of those small, incremental changes.

14

The Subtlety of Ignoring Judgement

Living here in South Italy has taught me a lot about personal growth and one of the most important lessons is how to handle judgement. Let's start with a hard truth: judgement is everywhere. It's that little voice in your head—or more often, someone else's voice—telling you that you're not enough or that you should be doing things differently. This feeling of knowing better, even when you don't, is the essence of judgement. It creeps up on us, often masked as concern or advice, but at its core, it's a form of ignorance.

Whether it's about your career, your relationships or your personal growth, judgement is always lurking, ready to pounce.

Judgement often stems from a place of insecurity. It's a way for people to deflect from their own shortcomings by highlighting what they perceive as flaws in others. It's a defence mechanism, a way of elevating oneself by stepping on someone else's toes. Let's be honest, we've all been there—feeling better about ourselves by pointing out someone else's mistakes or differences.

Take my own experiences with judgement on YouTube, for example. I've faced comments about my language learning and my portrayal of life in South Italy. At first, I felt compelled to defend myself, to rationalise and justify every move I made. Over time though, I realised that these judgments were rooted in ignorance. The people leaving those comments didn't know the full story of my life or the efforts I've made. Their judgments were reflections of their own insecurities.

Judgement is irrelevant. It doesn't matter if someone thinks you're not doing things right or if they criticise your choices. What matters is that you stay true to yourself and your path. As humans we are all intrinsically the same, with the same basic needs and experiences. The pedestal that judgement places others on is often built on shaky ground.

Remember, judgement is not about you—it's about the person judging. They're projecting their own insecurities and frustrations onto you. When you understand this, it becomes easier to ignore their opinions. In the grand scheme of life, we're all on our own unique journeys.

So, how do you handle judgement? The first step is to acknowledge it for what it is—an attempt by someone else to distract from their own issues. Next, focus on your own journey. If you're doing something bold or unconventional, expect criticism. It's a natural part of breaking free from societal norms and expectations.

When judgement comes your way, don't let it derail you. Use it as a sign that you're on the right path. People often judge what they don't understand or what threatens their own comfort zones. If you're pushing boundaries, you're likely doing something noteworthy.

Finally, choose your responses wisely. Not every comment or critique deserves your attention. Sometimes, the best response is no response. Focus on your goals and the progress you're making. Let the judgement roll off like water on a duck's back. Your journey is yours alone and it's worth every step, regardless of what others think.

Judgement is an inevitable part of life, especially when you're making bold moves or taking unconventional paths. Don't let it hold you back. Embrace your journey, stay true to yourself, and remember that judgement says more about the judge than it does about you. Keep moving forward and don't let the noise of judgement distract you from your path.

Key Takeaways

1. **Judgement is a Reflection of Others' Insecurities.** Judgement isn't about you—it's about the person doing the judging. It often stems from their own insecurities and shortcomings. When someone criticises you, it's more a reflection of their internal struggles than a true assessment of your actions.
2. **Stay True to Your Own Journey**. Everyone's journey is unique, and so is their pace. If you're pursuing something unconventional or taking your time to achieve your goals, expect some criticism. The key is to stay true to your own path, regardless of external opinions.
3. **Not All Criticism Deserves a Response.** You don't have to engage with every piece of criticism you receive. Often, it's best to choose your battles and focus on constructive feedback that genuinely helps you to grow.

Actionable Tips

- **Remind yourself that it's not a measure of your worth.** Instead of getting defensive, take a moment to empathise with the judge's perspective. Then, refocus on your own path and objectives. Their opinion is their issue, not yours.
- **Set personal milestones and celebrate them, no matter how small they may seem.** Keep a journal of your progress and the reasons behind your choices. When faced with criticism, revisit your goals and remind yourself why you started this journey. Let your achievements be your guide, not the opinions of others.
- **Develop a filter for evaluating feedback.** Ask yourself if the criticism is constructive or if it's just noise. For comments that don't serve your growth, practise the art of ignoring them. This frees up mental space to focus on positive influences and productive feedback.

15

The Marathon of Life

It's a question that many of us grapple with at different points in our lives—should we approach our goals with the relentless speed of a sprinter or the steady, deliberate pace of a marathon runner?

Let's start with the sprint mindset. It's the exhilarating rush to achieve a goal, to cross that finish line as quickly as possible. It's the thrill of setting a target and racing towards it with all your might. We've all experienced it, whether it's in our career ambitions, personal projects or even day-to-day tasks. The sprint feels intense and immediate, promising the satisfaction of quick wins and instant results.

However, there's a catch. This high-speed approach often comes with its own set of challenges. When we focus solely on the end goal, we can become so consumed by the race that we miss out on the nuances and subtleties that could enrich our journey. We might overlook opportunities, fail to notice the beauty around us or even neglect the gradual progress we're making. This sprinting mentality can lead to burnout, as we push ourselves too hard, too fast and find ourselves disillusioned when the finish line isn't as fulfilling as we had imagined.

Now, let's shift gears and explore the marathon mindset. Imagine a long, winding road stretching out before you. There's no rush, no immediate finish line in sight. Instead, there's a steady rhythm, a consistent pace that allows you to build endurance and appreciate the journey. This is the essence of the marathon approach—slow, steady and purposeful.

Adopting a marathon mindset means committing to the process, understanding that meaningful progress takes time. It's about setting a foundation that can weather storms, making small, incremental improvements and finding joy in the journey itself. This approach encourages us to savour the moments, learn from the experiences and build something that has real depth and value. It's the slower, more deliberate path, but it's one that often leads to more sustainable success and greater satisfaction.

Should we exclusively embrace the marathon mindset or can we incorporate elements of the sprint into our approach? The truth is, it's about finding a balance. There are times when sprinting towards a goal can be beneficial, providing the drive and urgency needed to overcome immediate challenges. However, it's equally important to recognise when to shift into marathon mode, to take a step back and to appreciate the journey.

For instance, when I started my YouTube channel, I was tempted by the allure of instant success. I wanted to see rapid growth and immediate results, but the reality of building a channel is that it's a marathon. It requires patience, persistence and a steady approach. The incremental improvements, the slow build-up of subscribers and the gradual enhancement of content quality are all part of a process that takes time. Now, as I look back, I appreciate the journey and the growth that came with it much more than if I had experienced a quick surge of success.

One of the most profound realisations on this marathon journey is that the destination often feels anticlimactic. We spend so much time fixating on the end goal, thinking that reaching it will bring us ultimate happiness. Yet, the real magic often lies in the journey itself—the effort, the growth and the transformation.

In language learning, for example, many people expect to achieve fluency in record time. However, mastering a language is a marathon, not a sprint. It requires time, practice and immersion. The process of learning and gradually improving can be incredibly rewarding, offering insights and skills that go beyond just speaking the language.

Similarly, in our careers and personal lives, embracing the marathon mindset allows us to build a solid foundation. It prepares us to handle challenges, seize opportunities and sustain our success over the long term. It's about understanding that while the end goal is important, the journey we take to get there is where we find true value and growth.

As you navigate your own journey, consider how you can blend the urgency of the sprint with the steadiness of the marathon. Recognise the times when a sprint might be necessary to achieve a specific goal, but also appreciate the moments when a marathon approach will provide the depth and sustainability you need.

Ultimately, the marathon of life is about more than just reaching the finish line. It's about how you run the race, how you experience the path and how you grow along the way. Embrace the journey, cherish the progress, and find fulfilment in both the milestones and the moments in between.

Key Takeaways

1. **Embrace the Journey, Not Just the Destination.** The real value often lies in the journey itself rather than the end goal. While reaching milestones is important, the process of getting there offers the most profound growth and satisfaction.
2. **Balance Sprinting with Marathon Thinking.** Both sprinting and marathon approaches have their place. Learn to recognise when it's time to push hard towards a short-term goal and when it's better to adopt a slower, more deliberate pace for long-term success.
3. **Build a Strong Foundation for Long-Term Success.** Building a solid foundation through steady, incremental efforts can help you handle challenges better and seize opportunities when they arise. Quick wins are great, but a well-established base ensures lasting success.

Actionable Tips

- **Set Milestones.** Break down your larger goals into smaller, manageable milestones. Celebrate each achievement to stay motivated and appreciate your progress.
- **Reflect Regularly.** Take time to reflect on what you're learning and experiencing along the way. Keep a journal to capture insights

and moments of growth.

- **Practise Mindfulness.** Engage fully in each step of your journey. Practise mindfulness techniques to stay present and enjoy the process rather than rushing to the finish line.
- **Prioritise Tasks.** Identify tasks that require immediate action and those that benefit from a long-term approach. Allocate your energy accordingly.
- **Set Time Limits.** Use sprinting techniques for short-term projects or tasks by setting deadlines and focusing intensively during those periods.
- **Schedule Downtime.** Incorporate periods of rest and reflection into your routine to recharge and ensure you're maintaining a steady, sustainable pace over time.

16

Performing Monkey Syndrome

The term "Performing Monkey Syndrome" is my way of describing those moments when we find ourselves in roles and situations that don't quite fit—yet we feel compelled to play along. You know the drill: you're doing something that feels uncomfortable, out of sync with your true self, but there's this nagging sense of obligation or expectation. It's like you're on stage, performing a part that isn't really you.

We've all been there. Perhaps you took on a task at work that wasn't in your job description or maybe you agreed to plans you'd rather avoid, all because you didn't want to disappoint someone or risk looking bad. It's a dance many of us learn early on: doing things we don't want to do, in order to keep up appearances or to please others.

So, why do we find ourselves in this exhausting performance? I believe there are two primary reasons:

1. **The Need for Approval**: We all want to be seen in a positive light. There's something deeply ingrained in us that craves admiration and approval from others. We put ourselves in situations we're

not comfortable with, hoping to create a favourable impression, even if it means stretching ourselves thin.

2. **The Desire to Please**: Another strong driver is our wish to make others happy. We often think that if we bend over backwards to accommodate others, they'll value us more or appreciate us better. Yet, this often comes at a steep personal cost.

Recently, I found myself caught in a situation where I was very much the Performing Monkey. Despite my best efforts to set boundaries, I ended up doing something that made me feel deeply uncomfortable. At that moment, I thought it was the right thing to do—there was an unspoken expectation and I feared how others would view me if I didn't comply.

Afterwards, I felt awful. It was like trying to fit into shoes that were two sizes too small. I was upset with myself and it took some reflection to realise that I had let myself slip into that Syndrome. The core realisation? I had been chasing approval and trying to please others, at the expense of my own well-being.

It's not just personal interactions where this Syndrome plays out. Society, with its myriad of expectations, can be a huge contributor. We are bombarded with messages about how we should be creating content, achieving milestones or living our lives. These societal pressures can push us into Performing Monkey Mode, where we're more focused on meeting external expectations than on staying true to ourselves.

It's easy to get swept up in the idea that success looks a certain way or that there's a right way to do things. Here's the kicker: what truly matters is whether those actions are in alignment with who you are and what you genuinely want. Striving to meet society's standards at the expense of your happiness is a recipe for dissatisfaction.

So, how do you escape this cycle? It starts with boundaries. It's about learning to say "no" and sticking to your guns when you feel something isn't right for you. Boundaries are not just about physical limits; they're about emotional and psychological ones as well.

Reflect on the situations where you've felt like a Performing Monkey. Ask yourself: "Was this really what I wanted to do?" If the answer is no, then it's time to reassess things, so you don't keep yourself stuck in this Mode.

Remember, your happiness and alignment with your true self should be your guiding light. It's perfectly okay to prioritise your own needs and well-being. If that means disappointing someone or stepping back from an obligation, so be it. The only person you're guaranteed to spend every moment with is yourself and the relationship you have with yourself is the single most important one.

Life is too short to be stuck in roles that don't fit or to chase after approval that ultimately doesn't bring you joy. Embrace what makes you feel good and align your actions with your true self. If you find yourself performing, ask yourself: "Is this something I would choose if I had the freedom to decide?" If it's not, then give yourself permission to step away.

It's important to focus on living authentically and setting boundaries that protect our sense of self. Life will always have its demands and expectations, but you don't have to lose yourself in the process. Reclaim your identity, honour your own needs and let go of the Performing Monkey Syndrome.

Your true self will thank you for it.

Key Takeaways

1. **Understand the Performing Monkey Syndrome.** The Performing Monkey Syndrome involves engaging in activities that don't align with your true self due to perceived obligations or external expectations. It's a common trap where we prioritise others' opinions over our own comfort and authenticity.
2. **Prioritise Your Own Needs and Boundaries.** Setting and maintaining personal boundaries is crucial for wellbeing. Your happiness and alignment with your true self should always be a priority over meeting others' expectations or seeking approval.
3. **Focus on Authenticity and Self-Alignment.** Authenticity is key to a fulfilling life. Align your actions with what truly makes you happy and who you really are, rather than conforming to societal pressures or external expectations.

Actionable Tips

- **Regularly check in with yourself.** When faced with a new task or request, ask, "Does this feel right for me?" If it doesn't align with your values or comfort, acknowledge that it's okay to say no or to set boundaries. This self-awareness will help you avoid slipping into the Performing Monkey role.
- **Practise asserting your boundaries.** Start by saying no to requests that stretch you too thin or make you uncomfortable. Focus on smaller, manageable situations to build your confidence.

Remember, saying no is a form of self-respect and an important step in preserving your personal integrity.

- **Reflect on your current commitments and activities**. Evaluate whether they genuinely bring you joy or if they are being done to meet others' expectations. Make adjustments to focus more on activities that resonate with your true self. Prioritise pursuits that light you up and contribute to your overall happiness and fulfillment.

17

Dare to Detach

Detachment is more than just an abstract concept; it's a vital skill for navigating life's unpredictable tides.

Picture life as a vast ocean filled with shifting currents and unforeseen storms. Without detachment, you're at the mercy of those elements, tossed around by every wave and gust of wind. However with detachment, you become the skilled sailor who remains steady, regardless of the chaos around you.

This skill allows you to maintain your inner peace and stability. When you master detachment, you no longer let external variables—be they people, situations or even your own fluctuating emotions—dictate your inner state. You become resilient, finding calm in the midst of the storm.

In today's world, practising detachment is easier said than done. We live in an era dominated by instant feedback and constant validation, largely driven by social media. Our lives are intertwined with platforms designed to elicit quick emotional responses—likes, comments, shares. The dopamine hits we receive from these interactions can make it incredibly challenging to stay detached.

We're wired to react to external stimuli. It's almost instinctive. We crave recognition and approval, which makes it difficult to resist the urge to let others' opinions shape how we feel about ourselves and our work. The key is to recognise this pattern and consciously choose to step back.

Consider toxic environments—be it a toxic job, a strained relationship or even a challenging family dynamic. These situations are characterised by unpredictable swings between positive and negative experiences. One day you're valued and appreciated; the next, you feel drained and undervalued. This inconsistency is emotionally taxing.

Practising detachment doesn't mean you disengage or become apathetic. It means you maintain your emotional equilibrium despite the turbulence around you. It's about understanding that while you may not be able to change the environment, you can control your response to it. Detachment becomes your anchor, allowing you to stay centred and focused on what truly matters.

People are complex and often act out of their own insecurities and unresolved issues. Their behaviour, especially when negative or nonsensical, is a reflection of their own struggles rather than a true measure of your worth. This is particularly true in online environments where anonymity can embolden people to act out in hurtful ways.

By practising detachment, you can prevent others' words and actions from impacting your self-esteem or emotional state. Recognise that hurtful comments or actions often stem from the other person's discontent. You don't need to internalise their negativity. Instead, choose to maintain your own positive and focused mindset.

Detachment is not about ignoring reality or avoiding difficult situations. It's about empowering yourself to remain unaffected by factors beyond your control. When you embrace detachment, you reclaim your personal power. You stop being a passive participant in life's drama and become the master of your own emotional landscape.

Imagine a life where your mood isn't dictated by others' actions or opinions. Envision yourself moving through challenges with a calm demeanour, unaffected by the chaos that might have previously thrown you off course. This is the freedom that detachment brings.

Detachment is a journey, not a destination. It requires ongoing practice and self-awareness. As you work on integrating detachment into your life, you'll find that it becomes a valuable tool for coping with the ups and downs of existence. You'll navigate relationships and situations with greater ease, finding peace amid the uncertainty.

Remember, practising detachment is about preserving your own wellbeing and focusing on what truly matters to you. It's about choosing to rise above negativity and maintaining your own course. By doing so, you ensure that your dreams and personal aspirations remain undisturbed by the storms that may arise around you.

Embrace detachment as a way to safeguard your inner peace and create a life that's driven by your values and goals, not by the whims of external circumstances.

Key Takeaways

1. **Detachment Empowers Inner Stability**: Mastering detachment is crucial for maintaining emotional equilibrium. By not letting external variables—like people's opinions or situational fluctuations—control your feelings, you stay grounded and resilient.

2. **Modern Society Challenges Detachment:** In an age where instant feedback and social media dictate much of our emotional landscape, practising detachment becomes essential. It helps you navigate through the noise and maintain a sense of self-worth independent of external validation.

3. **Detachment is a Coping Mechanism for Toxic Environments**: Whether dealing with toxic work conditions, challenging relationships or negative online interactions, detachment allows you to manage your responses and protect your emotional well-being. It's about staying centred even when external circumstances are less than ideal.

Actionable Tips

- **Set Boundaries with Social Media**. Limit your exposure to platforms that trigger emotional highs and lows. Allocate specific times for checking social media and be mindful of how interactions affect your mood. Use apps that track your screen time to help maintain these boundaries.

- **Practise Mindfulness and Self-Reflection**. Incorporate mindfulness exercises into your daily routine to strengthen your ability to detach from external stressors. Techniques like meditation, journaling or deep-breathing exercises can help you maintain a calm and centred mindset.

- **Reframe Negative Feedback**. When faced with criticism or negativity, consciously reframe the situation. Recognise that such feedback often reflects the other person's issues rather than your own worth. Challenge negative thoughts by reminding yourself of your strengths and achievements.

18

Press Pause

We live in a world that glorifies constant hustle. The narrative we've been fed is that we need to work relentlessly, seizing every opportunity and pushing ourselves to the brink. It's easy to get caught up in this whirlwind of productivity and ambition, but here's a truth I've come to understand: living this way can lead to burnout. I've been there and it's not pretty.

When I was running my own business, I was practically working seven days a week. My days were filled from dawn till dusk with tasks and to-dos. I was on the brink of burnout more times than I'd like to admit. It's especially tempting to overwork when you're passionate about what you do, as the lines between work and pleasure blur, but passion doesn't protect you from exhaustion. It's precisely because you love what you do that you need to set firm boundaries.

I had a profound realisation about this just recently. I allowed myself a full day of doing absolutely nothing productive—just a day in pyjamas. Now, that's something that's incredibly rare for me. My usual routine is packed with activities: waking up between 5:30 and 6:00 a.m., indulging in my morning practices—gratitude rituals, Italian study, tapping, reflecting on my vision board and so on. Every moment of my day is meticulously planned to maximise productivity, even when it comes to my passion projects like my YouTube channel and personal brand.

On that pyjama day though, I embraced stillness and allowed myself to engage in activities completely unrelated to work—watching videos, listening to podcasts just for fun and letting my mind wander. It felt liberating. It was a stark reminder of the importance of slowing down, not as a last resort when you're exhausted, but as a deliberate practice to maintain balance.

This brings me to a crucial point: the importance of setting boundaries and creating space for self-care. I've decided that Sundays are my "fill my cup" days—a time dedicated to recharging and enjoying life outside of work. Whether it's reading a book, going for a walk, spending time with others or simply soaking up the sun, this day is about nourishing myself without any work-related distractions. It's about replenishing my energy so that I can face the upcoming week with renewed vigour.

We often get so caught up in the demands of life—work, family, responsibilities—that we forget to refill our own cup. If we don't take time to restore our energy, we end up running on empty, which affects not just ourselves but everyone around us. Boundaries are essential; they protect our energy and ensure that we don't deplete ourselves for others.

So, let this chapter serve as a gentle reminder: give yourself permission to press pause. It's not just about avoiding burnout; it's about enriching your life and maintaining your wellbeing. Find joy in the mundane, savour the little moments that bring you happiness, and remember that you're here to experience life fully—not just to work.

As you move forward, try to integrate moments of stillness and relaxation into your routine. Whether it's a full day, half a day or just an hour, dedicate time to activities that fill you up and make you feel good. Embrace the balance between hustle and rest and watch how it transforms not just your productivity, but your overall joy and satisfaction in life.

Here's to a life where we cherish our pauses as much as our pursuits. After all, it's not just about striving and achieving; it's also about enjoying the journey and savouring the present moments that make it all worthwhile.

Key Takeaways

1. **Embrace the Necessity of Rest**. Constant hustle without breaks leads to burnout. Even if you're passionate about your work, setting aside time to rest is crucial for maintaining long-term productivity and well-being.
2. **Set Boundaries to Protect Your Energy.** Boundaries are essential to prevent burnout and ensure you have the energy to give your best in both personal and professional realms. They safeguard your wellbeing and help you maintain a healthy balance.
3. **Prioritise Self-Care and Personal Fulfillment.** Making time for activities that fill you up emotionally and spiritually is vital. Personal fulfillment and joy contribute to overall happiness and productivity.

Actionable Tips

- **Schedule Rest Periods.** Mark out specific times in your calendar dedicated solely to relaxation. It could be a full day, a half-day or even just a few hours each week.
- **Define Clear Boundaries.** Identify your limits in terms of work hours and personal time. Communicate these boundaries clearly to colleagues, clients and even family members.
- **Create a "Self-Care" List.** List activities that help you recharge, whether it's a day at the beach, trying a new recipe or simply watching your favourite shows. Refer to this list when planning your rest time.
- **Reflect and Adjust.** Periodically assess how well you're maintaining your balance between work and personal life. Make adjustments as needed to ensure that your routine continues to support your wellbeing and happiness.

19

Navigating the Amazon Culture

We live in an age where the term 'Amazon Culture' isn't just about the online retail giant but something that reflects a broader societal expectation: the idea that everything should be available to us, all the time, no matter the day or hour.

When I think of 'Amazon Culture', I imagine a world where the lines between work and personal time blur into a seamless expectation of availability. This mindset has trickled down from the convenience we've come to expect from Amazon itself– where you can order anything you need at any hour and have it delivered almost instantaneously. It's a marvel of modern logistics, no doubt, but it also sets a precedent that isn't always realistic or fair when applied to other professions.

A few months ago, during the Easter Holiday here in Italy, I found myself facing one such example of this Culture. Easter Monday, or Pasqua, is a public holiday in Italy yet despite this, I had students who seemed to expect English lessons as if it were any ordinary day of the week. It's fascinating how deeply the 'Amazon Culture' has seeped into our expectations. The idea that services should be available 24/7, regardless of traditional breaks or holidays, is a direct reflection of the convenience culture Amazon represents.

Let's take a step back and consider the reality of service professions like teaching. Teaching is not just about delivering content; it's a mentally demanding job that requires significant energy and focus. Unlike the robust infrastructure that supports Amazon's round-the-clock service, teaching lacks a similar support system. Teachers need time to recharge, just like anyone else, to maintain the quality of their service. The demand for constant availability, therefore, not only places undue pressure on teachers but can also compromise the quality of teaching they offer.

Artificial Intelligence is another factor that intensifies this on-demand expectation. AI systems can offer certain types of services round-the-clock, filling gaps where human availability is limited. However, while AI might handle tasks like language learning or customer service enquiries, it cannot replicate the nuanced, empathetic interaction that comes from human contact. The demand for immediacy and flexibility fuelled by technological advancements further embeds the 'Amazon Culture' into our daily lives, but we must remember that technology cannot replace the human touch.

As we navigate this era of instant gratification, it's crucial to balance our expectations with a respect for the human element behind the services we receive. Just as we value the convenience of on-demand services, we should also appreciate and respect the need for downtime and quality in the services provided by real people. A little empathy goes a long way, especially when it comes to understanding that not every sector can operate with the same level of flexibility as a tech giant like Amazon.

Next time you find yourself expecting immediate availability from a service provider, take a moment to reflect on the context. Is your request reasonable? Does it respect the person's need for rest and quality service? In an age where convenience is King, let's not lose sight of the human side of life. After all, it's our ability to rest, recharge and maintain our wellbeing that ultimately ensures we can deliver our best work.

Key Takeaways

1. **Understand the Limitations of Service Professions.** Not every profession is built to operate 24/7. While Amazon and similar tech giants have the infrastructure to support round-the-clock services, many jobs especially those involving human interaction like teaching, require downtime to maintain their quality.
2. **Recognise the Human Element Behind Services.** The ease and immediacy provided by technology should not overshadow the fact that many services are powered by real people who need rest and recuperation. Human providers are not machines and require downtime to perform effectively.
3. **Balance Convenience with Realistic Expectations.** The on-demand culture driven by technology offers incredible convenience but comes with the responsibility of balancing expectations with the realities of human capacity. Just because technology can provide instant access doesn't mean every aspect of life can or should.

Actionable Tips

- **Before making a request, consider whether it's reasonable given the context of the service.** For instance, if you're requesting a service on a public holiday, recognise that not everyone may be available. Acknowledge and respect their need for time off to ensure they can deliver their best work when they are available.
- **Approach service providers with empathy and understanding.** If you need to schedule something, plan ahead and allow flexibility in your request. This not only shows respect for their time but also ensures that when you do receive service, it's delivered with full attention and quality.
- **Reflect on whether your expectations align with the service provider's capacity.** When interacting with human service providers, consider their workload and the possibility of delays and plan accordingly.

20

Mastering Haters

When you step into the public domain, whether it's through a blog, YouTube channel or any other platform, you're essentially opening a door to a world where anyone can express their opinions about you. It's like throwing a party and discovering that some of your guests are there just to critique the decorations or complain about the music. This is an inevitable part of the public arena—a reality that every content creator, influencer or public figure encounters.

Over my three years running a YouTube channel, I've seen my fair share of criticism. It's a phenomenon that is as universal as it is amusing. The most amusing part? Many of these critics, the so-called trolls and haters, would never dare to say such things to your face in real life. There's a certain irony in that, isn't there?

One of the most insightful quotes I've come across on this topic goes something like "I don't let trolls bother me because I'm grateful I don't have to deal with them in real life." How true is that? Behind a screen, people feel emboldened to unleash their negativity, a luxury they wouldn't have if they had to face you in person. This realisation can be a comforting reminder: you're dealing with keyboard warriors who, in reality, would likely never confront you directly.

Criticism is a double-edged sword. On one hand, there are comments that genuinely help you improve—like feedback on the audio quality of a video or suggestions for better content. I've found that these types of comments, while sometimes harsh, can be a goldmine for growth. They're like a mirror reflecting areas where you can enhance your craft.

On the other hand, there are comments that exist purely to challenge your experiences or opinions, often based on outdated beliefs or misinformation. These types of criticisms are less about constructive feedback and more about sowing seeds of doubt. It's crucial to recognize the difference and focus on what you can change for the better, while letting go of what's simply noise.

Understanding the circle of influence is key to managing how you respond to negativity. There are aspects of your life and work that you can control—your reactions, your responses and the content that appears on your platform. Trolls and haters fall outside this circle. You can't control them, no matter how much you might want to convince them of your perspective. What you can control, however, is how you manage your own environment and how you respond to these external pressures.

This is where the power of boundaries comes into play. For example, you have the authority to decide what content stays on your channel and what gets deleted. By maintaining this control, you create an environment that reflects your values and standards, rather than letting negativity dictate the atmosphere.

Every time you encounter negativity, think of it like a mosquito bite—irritating but manageable. Instead of letting it fester, respond with positivity. People who engage in trolling are often driven by their own dissatisfaction and bitterness. They thrive on creating conflict. By countering their negativity with love and light, you not only disarm them but also reinforce the positive environment you wish to cultivate.

Remember, when you are in a good place, you don't have the urge to spew negativity. It's usually those who are struggling who resort to such behaviour. So, when faced with unkind comments, treat them as an opportunity to practise compassion and maintain your own inner peace.

Ultimately, how you respond to negativity teaches others how to treat you. By setting clear boundaries—whether that means deleting offensive comments or walking away from heated confrontations—you establish a standard for how you expect to be treated. This self-respect is not just about protecting your space but also about reinforcing the value of your work and your wellbeing.

Focus on what you can control: your reactions, your content and your boundaries. Let go of what you cannot change and use every interaction as a chance to reinforce the positivity and resilience that define your journey.

In the end, it's not about eliminating criticism but mastering the art of responding with grace and confidence. As you continue to share your voice and passion with the world, remember that you have the power to shape the conversation and maintain the environment you want.

Key Takeaways

1. **Understand the Nature of Online Criticism.** Many online critics wouldn't dare to express their negativity face-to-face. Their behaviour is often emboldened by the anonymity of the internet.
2. **Differentiate Between Constructive Feedback and Unconstructive Noise.** Constructive criticism can help you grow, while unconstructive comments are often just noise meant to stir up negativity.
3. **Control Your Reactions and Maintain Your Circle of Influence.** You can't control others' opinions or actions, but you can control how you respond and what content remains visible on your social platforms.

Actionable Tips

- **View Criticism with Perspective.** Remind yourself that online negativity often comes from a place of anonymity and doesn't reflect how people would behave in real life. Whenever you encounter harsh comments, remember the source's limitations and keep your focus on constructive feedback.
- **Filter and Reflect.** Identify which comments provide actionable feedback that you can use to improve your work. Use these insights to make enhancements. For comments that are purely critical without substance or are meant to provoke, don't hesitate to delete or ignore them. Protect your creative space by keeping it positive.
- **Manage Your Response.** Cultivate a practice of responding to negativity with positivity or detachment. Show empathy but don't let negativity affect your mood or work.

21

The Magic of Mornings

There's something transformative about waking up before the world fully awakens. The early hours of the morning, when the sun is just beginning to paint the sky with hues of pink and gold, hold a certain magic that's hard to describe but easy to feel. The streets are still, the air is crisp and the only sounds are the gentle chirping of birds—a stark contrast to the chaos of daily life that comes later.

I never considered myself a true early bird until I moved to South Italy. Sure, I've always leaned towards waking up early, even during my time in the UK, but it was more out of necessity than desire. My life was structured around the demands of work and routine, with early mornings often forced upon me by schedules that left little room for leisure. Here in Palermo though, something shifted. My body naturally began to rise with the sun, waking me up at 5:30am or 6:00 am daily, even on Sundays. The funny thing is, what once felt like a chore has now become a much loved ritual.

It's hard to explain to someone who isn't an early riser why this time of day is so special. For many, the comfort of bed in the early hours is the ultimate luxury—who needs to get up at 5 or 6 a.m. when you could be cosy under the covers? However if you've never given early mornings a proper chance, you're missing out on an experience that can truly reshape your life.

My journey into becoming an early bird began when I worked in Naples. Back then, I used to wake up at 4am every day just to catch the train and start my commute. Those were tough times, I won't lie. I was often exhausted by the time I got home, drained by the demands of the day. Even during that gruelling period, there was something about the early hours that resonated with me, something that called me back to it even after those challenging days were behind me.

Now, my mornings are different. Waking up at 5:30 or 6:00 am feels like a gift I give myself each day. It's not just about getting up early—it's about what I do with that time. I've crafted a morning routine that aligns with my energy levels and allows me to feel accomplished before the day truly begins. Before I've even set foot outside my door, I've already achieved something, whether it's having read a book, completed a gratitude practice or simply having enjoyed a quiet cup of coffee while watching the sunrise.

Oh and that sunrise—it's something else. Every morning, the sky puts on a different show and every day feels like a fresh start. It's a gentle reminder that no matter what happened yesterday, today is a new day with new possibilities. I've come to believe that this sense of renewal is something we miss out on when we wake up later, rushing through our mornings in a blur of activities, barely grounded in the moment.

I understand that waking up early isn't for everyone. We all have different rhythms and what works for one person might not work for another, but I genuinely believe that there's something worth exploring in the quiet magic of the early morning. It's a time of day when you can truly connect with yourself before the world's demands start pulling you in different directions.

One of the most common reasons people give for not pursuing their dreams or working on their passions is that they don't have enough time. I've come to realise that it's not about having more time—it's about making the most of the time you already have. Waking up just 30 minutes earlier each day could be the key to unlocking those precious moments you've been longing for. You see it's not about the quantity of time you dedicate; it's about the consistency. Fifteen minutes of daily effort adds up to far more than sporadic bursts of energy. It's in the steady, regular practice that real progress is made.

Living in a busy city like Palermo, I've learnt to cherish the calm of the early morning. Once you step out into the world, the hustle and bustle can feel overwhelming, with cars honking and people rushing around. In those early hours, there's a peace that you rarely find at any other time of day. It's a moment to breathe, to centre yourself and to set the tone for whatever lies ahead.

So, if you're someone who's never tried waking up early, I encourage you to give it a go. Start small—maybe just 15 minutes earlier than usual—and see how it feels. Experiment with it, especially in the lighter, warmer months of spring and summer when waking up early becomes a bit easier. You might be surprised at how much it changes your perspective, how much more you can accomplish before the world wakes up. Who knows? You might just find yourself becoming a permanent early bird too!

Key Takeaways

1. **Embrace the Magic of Mornings**: The early hours offer a unique tranquillity and sense of renewal that can set a positive tone for your entire day.
2. **Consistency Over Quantity**: Small, regular efforts—like dedicating 15 minutes each morning to a goal—can lead to significant progress over time.
3. **Create Time, Don't Find It**: Waking up a little earlier can give you the extra minutes you need to pursue your passions and achieve your goals.

Actionable Tips

- **Start Small**. If waking up early feels daunting, try setting your alarm just 15 minutes earlier than usual. Gradually increase the time as your body adjusts.
- **Craft a Morning Routine**. Design a routine that aligns with your energy levels in the morning. It could include activities like stretching, meditation, journaling or simply enjoying a quiet moment with your thoughts.
- **Celebrate the Sunrise**. Take a moment each morning to watch the sunrise or step outside to breathe in the fresh morning air. Use this time to reflect on the new day and set your intentions.

22

If you only choose one book

There is one book, in particular, that has had a profound impact on me—a book that has not only inspired me but also transformed the way I approach life. That book is *Atomic Habits* by James Clear.

It was a few years ago when I first picked up this gem and I must admit, I was sceptical. I had read countless self-help books before, many of which were filled with motivational fluff but lacked the depth and practicality needed to make real, lasting change. *Atomic Habits* was different. From the very first page, I could sense that this was more than just another self-improvement book; it was a blueprint for real, tangible change.

The core of *Atomic Habits* is built around a simple yet incredibly powerful concept: the 1% principle. It's the idea that if you focus on getting just 1% better every day, those small, seemingly insignificant improvements will compound over time, leading to remarkable progress. Imagine this: by the end of a year, you could be 365% better than when you started. It's a principle that is both empowering and accessible to everyone, regardless of where you are in life or what you want to achieve.

This idea resonated with me on a deep level. I think about how many times we've all set big, audacious goals for ourselves—whether it's getting fit, learning a new skill or improving our relationships—only to feel overwhelmed by the sheer magnitude of the task. We start with enthusiasm but quickly fizzle out when the results don't come as quickly as we'd hoped. What if, instead of focusing on the end goal, we shifted our attention to just being 1% better each day? What if we allowed ourselves to make small, incremental changes, knowing that they would add up to something truly significant?

At the heart of *Atomic Habits*, James Clear emphasises the importance of systems. Your habits, he argues, are only as good as the systems you put in place to support them. This was a game-changer for me. It made me rethink how I structure my day, how I manage my time and how I approach the tasks that fill my life. I began to see that the habits I wanted to cultivate weren't just about willpower or motivation; they were about creating systems that made it easier to do the things I wanted to do and harder to do the things I didn't.

If you want to eat healthier, for example, it's not just about resisting the temptation of junk food; it's about creating a system where healthy eating is the path of least resistance. Maybe that means meal prepping on Sundays, keeping fresh fruit and vegetables at eye level in your fridge or setting a reminder on your phone to drink more water throughout the day. By designing your environment to support your goals, you make it easier to stick to the habits that will lead you to success.

As I sit here now, I can't help but reflect on how this principle of 1% better has shaped my year so far. At this point in the year, many of us have either made significant strides toward our goals or have veered off course, feeling discouraged and out of alignment with the intentions we set at the start of the year. Here's the thing: it's never too late to course-correct. It's never too late to start making those 1% improvements.

Reading *Atomic Habits* has reminded me that change doesn't have to be monumental or immediate. It can be gradual and steady. As long as you're moving in the right direction, those small steps will add up to something extraordinary and that's the beauty of it.

I really want to encourage you to embrace the 1% principle. Start small. Be patient with yourself. Create systems that support your goals and remember that every day is an opportunity to be just a little bit better than you were yesterday.

I also want to encourage you to read this book - it's a New York Times Bestseller for a very good reason!

Key Takeaways

1. **The Power of 1% Better Every Day.** Focus on making small, incremental improvements in your life. Over time, these tiny changes will compound into significant progress, transforming your life in ways you never imagined.
2. **Systems Over Goals.** Your habits are only as strong as the systems you put in place to support them. Design your environment and daily routines in a way that makes it easier to stick to positive habits and harder to fall into negative ones.
3. **Embrace Patience and Consistency.** Change doesn't have to be immediate or dramatic. By being patient and consistent, you allow those 1% improvements to build up over time, leading to lasting, meaningful change.

Actionable Tips

- **Start with One Small Habit.** Choose one small habit you'd like to cultivate. It could be something as simple as drinking a glass of water first thing in the morning or taking a five-minute walk each day. Focus on this habit for a month and track your progress.
- **Design Your Environment**. Identify the systems and environments that either support or hinder your habits. Make small adjustments to your surroundings that make it easier to stick to your desired habits, like placing a book on your nightstand if you want to read more.
- **Reflect and Adjust Weekly**. Set aside time each week to reflect on your progress. Ask yourself: What worked? What didn't? How can I adjust my systems to be more supportive of my goals? Use this reflection time to make small tweaks that keep you moving forward.

23

Returning to Where It All Began

As I stepped off the train in Salerno, a wave of nostalgia washed over me. This was the city that had shaped me, the first Italian city I called home. It was here, back in 2018, that my journey in South Italy began—a place where I would learn some of the most difficult yet valuable lessons of my life.

I spent four years living in Salerno and although I now live in Palermo, returning to Salerno felt like a warm embrace from a long-lost friend. The narrow streets, the familiar faces and the sea all welcomed me back as if no time had passed.

Salerno holds a special place in my heart. It's not just a city to me; it's a foundation. It's where I experienced profound personal growth, where I learnt how to navigate the challenges of living in a foreign country and where I truly began to understand who I am. This city provided me with the grounding I needed to thrive in South Italy and returning after two years away, was an emotional journey that reminded me of some important life lessons that I want to share with you.

Salerno was my starting point. When I first arrived, I was overwhelmed by the language, the culture and the sheer difference from anything I had ever known. Salerno became the place that grounded me. It taught me that we all have to start somewhere and those starting points are crucial for our growth.

In life, it's easy to get caught up in the end goal—the final picture of what we want to achieve. However, it's important to remember that reaching those goals is a process. There's a journey involved and that journey often begins with a single, sometimes small, step. For me, that step was moving to Salerno. It wasn't always easy, but it was the perfect place to begin my Italian adventure.

Salerno is a city that's well-connected to other parts of Italy. You're just a short boat ride from the Amalfi Coast and close to Naples, making it easy to explore and experience different parts of the country. When I moved there in 2018, it wasn't as well-known as it is now, but it was exactly what I needed—a place to learn, grow and find my footing. Even though I eventually moved on to new experiences in Palermo, I will always look back on Salerno as the city that gave me my start.

By early 2022 though, my life in Salerno had become mundane. I was doing the same things every day and I couldn't see how my life could look any different. That's when I knew it was time for a change. It wasn't that there was anything wrong with Salerno—it's a beautiful city—but I had outgrown it. I needed fresh experiences and a new environment to continue growing as a person. That's what inspired my move to Palermo.

One of the most important lessons I've learnt is that change is not just inevitable; it's essential. Many people struggle with change because it's uncomfortable. We get used to our routines and comfort zones and the idea of stepping out of them can be terrifying. I realised though that by staying in the same place and doing the same things, we stop living.

Looking back now, I see just how vital that change was. My life in Palermo is radically different from my life in Salerno and I've made so many improvements. I feel more grounded and more at home in South Italy than ever before. If I had stayed in Salerno, I would have eventually started to feel resentful and that would have tarnished my love for the city. By knowing when to move on, I've been able to keep my positive relationship with Salerno intact and I know I'll always want to return.

As counterintuitive as it may sound, sometimes you need to go backwards to move forwards. We often focus so much on the future— on where we're going and what we want to achieve—that we forget to reflect on how far we've actually come.

My recent trip to Salerno reminded me of this. Walking the streets I used to know so well, seeing the people I used to spend time with, it was like stepping back in time. In doing so, I was able to see just how much I've grown. I remembered the person I was when I first moved to Salerno—the challenges I faced, the lessons I learnt—and I realised how far I've come.

This reflection gave me a renewed sense of motivation to keep moving forward. It's easy to get caught up in the hustle and bustle of daily life, always looking ahead to the next goal, the next destination. Taking the time to look back can be incredibly powerful. It's a reminder of the progress you've made and the strength you've gained along the way. Sometimes, revisiting the past is exactly what you need to propel yourself into the future.

Key Takeaways

1. **Embrace Your Starting Point:** No matter where you are in life, remember that everyone begins somewhere. Your starting point is not your final destination, but it's an essential part of your journey.
2. **Don't Be Afraid of Change:** Change is necessary for growth. If you're feeling stuck or stagnant, it might be time to make a change, even if it's uncomfortable. Recognize when it's time to move on, and trust that new experiences will bring new opportunities for growth.
3. **Reflect to Propel Forward:** Sometimes, the best way to move forwards is to look backwards. Reflecting on your past can give you the perspective you need to keep progressing. Don't be afraid to revisit old places or reconnect with people from your past—it can be a powerful tool for growth.

Actionable Tips

- **Take some time to journal about your starting point.** Where were you a few years ago? What challenges did you face? How have you grown since then?
- **Identify one area of your life where you feel stuck.** What small change could you make to shake things up? It could be as simple as trying a new hobby or as significant as considering a move.
- **Plan a visit to a place that holds significance for you.** It could be a city, a neighbourhood or even just a park where you used to

spend time. Use the visit as an opportunity to reflect on how far you've come and what your next steps might be.

24

The Education Trap

Life in South Italy offers a unique blend of beauty and complexity. The landscapes are stunning, the culture is rich, but living here presents challenges that you might not experience when only visiting. One such issue I've observed, especially among the younger generation, is what I call 'The Education Trap'. It's a situation that keeps many people stuck in a cycle of endless studying, with little to show for it in terms of real-life experience or career advancement.

Italy is a country that places an enormous emphasis on education. Degrees are not just a qualification; they are a status symbol. It's not uncommon to meet people in their late 20s or even early 30s who are still at university, pursuing yet another qualification in the hopes of improving their job prospects. Coming from the UK, where it's more typical to enter the workforce in your early 20s, this has been a strange phenomenon to wrap my head around.

The root of this issue is multifaceted. On one hand, you have students who are genuinely uncertain about what they want to do with their lives. They stay in the academic world, hoping that the next course, the next degree, will provide clarity. On the other hand, there are those who fear the job market—a fear that is not entirely unfounded. In Italy, many public jobs are secured through what is known as the *Concorso*, a public competition that is fiercely competitive with very few positions available. In some cases, thousands of candidates may compete for just a handful of jobs. Given these odds, it's no wonder that so many young people prefer to stay in the safe, familiar environment of academia.

However there's a significant downside to this approach. When these students do finally graduate, they often find themselves lacking the practical, hands-on experience that employers are looking for. Sure, they might have an impressive array of degrees, but what they don't have is real-world experience—something that is increasingly valued in today's job market. The truth is, employers are not just looking at your qualifications; they're looking at what you can actually do and how you've applied your knowledge in real-world situations.

So why don't more young people gain this experience while they're studying? The reasons are twofold. First, many families in Italy are willing to financially support their children well into adulthood, particularly while they are still studying. While this can be a blessing, allowing students to focus entirely on their studies, it also removes the necessity for them to work while they are at university. As a result, many miss out on valuable work experience and the financial independence that comes with it.

Secondly, even when opportunities for practical experience, such as internships, are available, they are often unpaid or pay so little that it's impossible to live off the income. This is particularly demotivating when you consider that these internships often require students to work as hard as full-time employees, but without the corresponding pay. It's a vicious cycle—students need experience to get a job, but the avenues available for gaining that experience are not always feasible.

What's more, staying in academia for too long can actually be detrimental to your future prospects. At some point, the very thing you think is setting you apart—your education—becomes the thing that holds you back. Employers may see a long academic history without work experience as a red flag, questioning why someone hasn't gained more real-world skills. This is 'The Education Trap': the longer you stay in it, the harder it is to get out.

Let's be clear, I'm not saying education isn't important. It is, but it's not the only thing that's important. Life is about more than just what you learn in a classroom. It's about how you apply that knowledge, how you interact with others and how you handle yourself in the real world. Those are the skills that will set you apart, not just the degrees you've earned.

Take me, for example. By the time I was 24, I was a Police Officer and by 30, I had started my own business. I gained skills in those roles that no university course could have ever taught me—skills like communication, discipline, empathy and the ability to think on my feet. I don't say this to boast, but to illustrate that there's a whole world of learning that happens outside of academia and it's this learning that often makes the difference between success and failure in life.

In Italy, there's an unspoken snobbery when it comes to qualifications. People with degrees are often held in higher regard, while those without are looked down upon. A degree doesn't make a person. Some of the most successful people in the world don't have degrees and yet they've built incredible careers based on their skills, their passions and their hard work. That's something to think about, especially if you find yourself stuck in 'The Education Trap'.

So, what's the solution? It's simple but not easy: you have to break free from the mindset that education alone is the key to your future. You have to be honest with yourself about what you're really gaining from staying in academia. Are you just studying for studying's sake, or is there a real purpose behind it? If not, it might be time to step out of the academic world and into the real one. Gain experience, develop skills and learn to stand on your own two feet. That's where true growth happens.

Key Takeaways

1. **Balance Education with Experience**: A degree is valuable, but it's not everything. Employers are looking for candidates with practical, real-world experience. Make an effort to gain this experience, even if it means taking on internships or part-time work while studying.
2. **Question Your Motivation:** Are you continuing your education because it's truly necessary for your career, or are you doing it out of fear or uncertainty? Be honest with yourself about why you're staying in academia.
3. **Seek Financial Independence**: Relying too much on family support can delay your personal growth and independence. Start thinking about how you can support yourself financially while still pursuing your education or career.

Actionable Tips

- **Consider freelance work.** If internships in your field are unpaid or low-paying, consider seeking out freelance work that can offer relevant experience.
- **Write down your career goals**. Map out a plan that includes both education and hands-on experience. If your education is no longer aligning with your goals, consider shifting your focus.
- **Create a budget.** Start managing your finances, even if you're still living at home. Look for ways to contribute to your living expenses or save for your future. This will help you build confidence and financial independence over time.

25

The Flake Factor

In the UK, we have a chocolate bar called Cadbury Flake. For those of you who aren't familiar with it, it's a delicious, crumbly treat that falls apart the moment you bite it. Some even argue it's not really a chocolate bar because it's so fragile and lacking in structure. Now, apply that same idea to a person's behaviour.

A flake is someone who crumbles under pressure, who says yes to something but backs out when the time comes, who can't seem to hold it together long enough to make a real decision or commitment. Let me tell you, I see a lot of this kind of behaviour here in South Italy.

You see, being a flake isn't just about indecision; it's about fear. Fear of making the wrong choice, fear of missing out on something better and ultimately, fear of failure. It's as if people are so terrified of committing to one path that they prefer to stay on the fence, never truly committing to anything. While they're stuck in this state of indecision, life moves on without them. Opportunities pass by and progress stalls.

I believe that flakiness is a shame, not only because it annoys others—

let's be real, no one likes to be let down—but also because it holds you back from living your best life. Imagine the potential that gets wasted when someone says "maybe" instead of "yes" or "no." Life is full of decisions and while it's natural to feel uncertain at times, letting that uncertainty control you will only lead to stagnation.

One of the things I've noticed is that this flaky behaviour often manifests in social commitments. People will agree to plans, but as the time draws near, they'll cancel at the last minute, leaving others in the lurch. Why? Maybe because they're holding out for something better or are blinded by the next bright, shiny object that promises more fun or excitement. Here's the truth though: life isn't about always finding the best option; it's about making the most of the options you choose.

I'm someone who does what I say I'm going to do. Now, I'm not perfect and I've learnt plenty of painful lessons along the way, but I've always believed that real progress comes from making a decision and sticking with it. That doesn't mean you can't adapt or pivot as you go—that's part of the journey—but you have to take that first step. You have to take action.

So many people don't. They stay stuck in indecision, blaming external circumstances like the government, the economy or their job situation. I've heard these excuses a million times and while I understand that these factors can make life difficult, they don't make it impossible.

What makes it impossible is refusing to act.

The most successful people, the ones we admire, didn't have all the answers when they started. They didn't wait for the perfect moment or the perfect opportunity. They took what they had, made a decision and committed to it. They took action, and through that action, they found their way.

So how can you overcome flakiness in your own life or deal with flaky people around you? First, if you recognise some of this behaviour in yourself, be honest. Ask yourself: How much progress have I really made? What have I missed out on because I couldn't commit? If you find that you've been turning down opportunities out of fear or uncertainty, it's time to take a long, hard look at your life and start making some changes.

Understand that failure isn't the enemy. Failure is a part of life and often, it's through failure that we find success. The problem with being a flake is that you avoid failure by avoiding decisions altogether and in doing so, you avoid success too. Instead of waiting for the perfect moment, commit to the opportunities in front of you. Say yes to the things that have potential, even if you're not 100% sure. You can figure out the details along the way.

If you're dealing with flaky people, don't let their behaviour drag you down. Recognise it for what it is—fear and uncertainty. Approach them with empathy, but also protect your own boundaries. Don't let their indecision impact your goals and dreams. Sometimes, the best thing you can do is to distance yourself and focus on your own path.

Key Takeaways

1. **Flakiness stems from fear and indecision.** People often avoid making decisions out of fear of failure or missing out, which ultimately leads to stagnation and missed opportunities.

2. **Commitment is crucial for progress.** Success comes from making decisions and sticking to them, even if the path isn't clear from the start. Progress is made through action, not inaction.
3. **Failure is not the enemy.** Embrace failure as a learning opportunity rather than something to be avoided. The road to success is often paved with mistakes and lessons learnt.

Actionable Tips

- **Start small with your commitments.** If you struggle with indecision, begin by committing to small, manageable tasks and follow through. Gradually build up your ability to commit to larger decisions.
- **Reframe your fear of failure.** Instead of seeing failure as a negative, view it as a necessary step towards growth and success. Each failure brings you closer to your goals.
- **Set clear boundaries with flaky people.** Recognise when others' indecision is affecting your life and take steps to protect your time and energy. It's okay to distance yourself from those who consistently let you down.

26

The Power of Saying No

In a world where social expectations and the desire to please others often tug at our sleeves, it's easy to lose sight of what truly matters to us. I recently had an epiphany that I believe will resonate with many of you: when you say yes to others, you're often saying no to yourself. This powerful realisation came to me after watching a thought-provoking YouTube video and it's something that has stuck with me ever since.

Let me paint a picture for you. Recently, I found myself in a situation that many of us face—juggling personal goals with social obligations. I had spent the entire Sunday in my pyjamas, deeply immersed in putting the final touches to my Salerno Travel Guide. This Guide, which had consumed weeks of my life, was now nearing completion and I had a deadline to meet. I was in the zone, laser-focused on finishing what I had started.

Then, as often happens in life, a last-minute social invitation arrived. The event was one of those typical spontaneous plans that often happen in South Italy. If I accepted, it would mean *at least* an hour of my time and I knew I couldn't just pop in and leave without seeming rude. I faced a choice: say yes to the social gathering or stay true to my commitment to finishing the Guide.

In that moment, I realised the importance of honouring my own commitments. If I said yes to the invitation, I would be saying no to myself and the work I had poured so much effort into. It's not about being selfish—though, let's face it, we all have a degree of selfishness within us. It's about respecting your own needs and goals, which are often overlooked in favour of pleasing others.

Here's the truth we often forget: when people ask for your time or attention, they're usually doing so with their own needs in mind, not yours. They may not consider how their request will impact your own priorities. This is why it's crucial to remain conscious of your own boundaries and commitments. It's easy to get sidetracked by the distractions of others, particularly when those distractions seem kind and well-meaning. However your goals and objectives deserve your attention, too.

Saying no isn't easy, especially in a culture where people expect a yes. It can feel harsh and there's often a sense of guilt that accompanies it, but no is a complete sentence. It doesn't require an elaborate explanation. It's a powerful tool for maintaining your boundaries and ensuring that you're focusing on what truly matters to you.

Consider this: when you say no to something that doesn't align with your goals, you're not just turning down an invitation or request. You're making space for what really matters—whether that's a project, a personal goal or simply the peace of mind that comes from not overcommitting yourself. Guess what? If people are offended or upset by your decision, it says more about their respect for you than it does about your choice.

In my case, saying no to the social invitation meant that I could complete my Travel Guide and achieve a goal I had set for myself. Let me tell you, there's nothing more satisfying than crossing something off your to-do list that you've worked so hard on. It's a reminder that prioritising yourself and your goals is not just okay—it's necessary.

Key Takeaways

1. **Your Goals Are a Priority**: When faced with competing demands, remember that your personal goals and commitments should come first. Saying no to others is sometimes the best way to say yes to yourself.
2. **No Is a Complete Sentence:** Don't feel obligated to justify your decisions. A simple no is often all that's needed to maintain your boundaries and focus on what's important to you.
3. **Respect Yourself to Earn Respect**: If others are offended by your choice to prioritise your own needs, it's a reflection of their respect for you. True friends will understand and support your decisions.

Actionable Tips

- **Set Clear Boundaries**. Define what you're willing to commit to in advance. This makes it easier to say no when new requests come in and helps you stay focused on your priorities.
- **Practise Assertiveness**. Work on delivering a confident and straightforward no. It doesn't require an explanation, but practising

how to say it can make the process easier and less uncomfortable.

- **Reflect on Your Priorities**. Regularly review your goals and commitments. This helps you stay aligned with what matters most and ensures you're not swayed by distractions or requests that don't serve your objectives.

27

The Power of Persistence

The day I brought Tina, my 10-week-old Border Collie puppy, home was one filled with excitement and a touch of nervous anticipation. She was a bundle of energy, curiosity and intelligence, all wrapped up in a small, furry package. Little did I know, this tiny creature would soon become one of my greatest teachers.

One afternoon, I decided to introduce Tina to a new toy—a plush animal, soft yet durable, designed to withstand the sharp teeth of a puppy. I watched as she eagerly grabbed the toy but what struck me wasn't her enthusiasm—it was her persistence.

Tina didn't just chew randomly on different parts of the toy; she focused on one specific spot, biting and tugging repeatedly. No matter how many times I threw the toy across the room or repositioned it, she always returned to the same spot. She was relentless in her pursuit, determined to make an impact on that one area.

This simple act of persistence was not just typical puppy behaviour; it was a reflection of a much larger principle. Tina wasn't successful in tearing the toy apart, but her determination was undeniable. She instinctively understood something that many of us often forget: persistence is key to achieving anything worthwhile.

That same morning, I had been reading about the distinction between fault and responsibility in the book, *The Subtle Art of Not Giving a F*ck* by Mark Manson. Manson's words echoed in my mind as I observed Tina's behaviour: "Fault is past tense; responsibility is present tense."

Fault is about the choices that have already been made—events that are out of our control. Responsibility, on the other hand, is about the choices we make in the here and now. It's about how we perceive situations, how we react and how we choose to move forward. This distinction is crucial because it shifts the focus from what has happened to what can happen, from blame to action.

Tina, of course, had no concept of fault or responsibility, but her actions embodied the essence of these ideas. She didn't give up when she didn't immediately succeed in tearing the toy apart. She didn't blame the toy for being too tough or quit after a few failed attempts. Instead, she kept at it, fully committed to the task at hand, living in the present and taking responsibility for her actions.

In life, many of us start with the best of intentions, filled with enthusiasm and dreams of success. When we don't see immediate results though or when the journey becomes more challenging than we had anticipated, it's easy to lose steam and give up. This is particularly true in today's fast-paced world, where instant gratification is often expected.

Take YouTube, for example. It's a platform that many people turn to with hopes of quick success—dreams of millions of followers, viral videos and lucrative sponsorships. However the reality is far different. Success on YouTube, much like in any other area of life, requires a significant amount of work, commitment and, most importantly, persistence.

Building a community on YouTube isn't about overnight success; it's about consistently creating content, engaging with your audience and staying true to your vision, even when the numbers don't immediately reflect your efforts. Unlike platforms like Instagram or TikTok, where quick likes and fleeting fame are more common, YouTube demands sustained effort. It's a place where you earn your audience's trust over time and the rewards, while slower to come, are often more substantial and meaningful.

This is why many aspiring YouTubers give up too soon. They start with excitement but falter when they realise the amount of work involved. The path to success is rarely a straight line; it's filled with ups and downs, moments of doubt and countless hours of work that go unseen. It's also filled with opportunities for growth, learning and ultimately, achievement—if you can stay persistent.

So, how do we apply these lessons from Tina's toy and Manson's book to our own lives? It starts with a mindset shift: moving from blame to responsibility. It's easy to blame external factors for what we don't have—a lack of time, resources or support - but blame keeps us stuck in the past, focusing on what went wrong instead of what can be done now.

Taking responsibility means accepting that we have the power to change our situation, even if the odds are stacked against us. It means understanding that while we can't control everything, we can control how we respond, how we adapt and how persistent we are in pursuing our goals.

Responsibility also involves being honest with ourselves about the work that needs to be done. Just like Tina with her toy, we need to focus on the task at hand, not getting distracted by quick fixes or easy outs. Persistence isn't just about working hard; it's about working smart, consistently and with purpose. It's about showing up every day, even when it's tough, even when progress seems slow and even when it feels like no one is watching.

As I continue to watch Tina grow, I'm reminded daily of the power of persistence. Her determination, her focus and her refusal to give up are qualities that I strive to embody in my own life. As I reflect on Manson's teachings, I see how responsibility and persistence are intertwined, each feeding into the other to create a life of purpose and achievement.

Life, like a plush toy in the hands of a determined puppy, will test us. It will challenge our resolve and our commitment to our goals. However if we can take responsibility for our choices and remain persistent in the face of obstacles, we will find that the journey, though difficult, is also incredibly rewarding.

Key Takeaways

1. **Persistence Is Essential for Success**: Whether in personal goals, career aspirations or new endeavours like starting a YouTube channel, persistence is the key to overcoming challenges and achieving meaningful results. Success often requires sustained effort and commitment over time, even when immediate results aren't visible.

2. **Responsibility Over Blame**: Shifting from a mindset of blaming external factors to taking responsibility for your current choices empowers you to make changes. Responsibility is about focusing on what you can do now to improve your situation, rather than dwelling on past mistakes or circumstances beyond your control.

3. **Consistency and Focus**: Achieving goals requires both consistency in your actions and a focused approach. Like Tina with her toy, targeting your efforts in specific areas and regularly working toward your objectives can lead to significant progress over time.

Actionable Tips

- **Set Small, Achievable Goals**. Break down your larger goals into smaller, more manageable tasks. This will make it easier to stay persistent, as each small win will build momentum and keep you motivated.

- **Practise Self-Reflection**. Regularly assess your progress and the choices you're making. Ask yourself if you're taking responsibility for your current situation and if there's anything you can do differently to move closer to your goals.

- **Focus on What You Can Control**. When faced with setbacks, shift your focus to the aspects of the situation that are within your control. Identify actions you can take to improve your circumstances rather than getting bogged down by things you can't change.

- **Celebrate Persistence, Not Just Results**: Acknowledge and reward yourself for staying committed to your goals, even if you haven't yet reached the finish line. Recognising your persistence helps maintain motivation.

28

The Power of Energy

In our fast-paced world, where appearances often take precedence over substance, there's a fundamental truth that we tend to overlook: energy is everything.

This isn't about the kind of energy that fuels our daily activities or keeps us going from one task to the next. No, I'm talking about the deeper, more subtle energy that permeates our interactions and environments— the kind of energy that speaks volumes beyond what words or actions can convey.

I've learnt over the years that tuning into this energy is not just an occasional skill but an essential practice for truly understanding the people and situations we encounter.

A few years ago, back in the UK, I went to a restaurant. It wasn't crowded, but there was something off. The energy was almost palpable, a strange undercurrent that told me this place was far from thriving. The air felt heavy and despite the physical appearance of the restaurant being decent, there was an unmistakable sense of unease. A few weeks later, my intuition was confirmed when I learnt that the restaurant had closed down. This wasn't a one-off occurrence. I've had similar experiences with both places and people. Smiles and kind words can be deceptive. The true energy behind them often reveals a different story.

Understanding and interpreting energy is not just about developing a keen sense of intuition; it's about recognising that this energy is a far more reliable indicator than any surface-level observation. We often become enamoured with polished appearances, but no matter how well-crafted the façade, it can't hide the underlying energy that subtly, yet powerfully, communicates the truth.

When assessing a situation or person, it's all too easy to rely on what we see and hear. However, those external factors can be manipulated. A business might boast a sleek design and a well-crafted website, but if the underlying energy is of struggle and uncertainty, that will seep through no matter how well the surface is maintained. It's the unchangeable energy that provides the most authentic insight.

In essence, energy is a pure, unalterable factor. It's something that people can't easily control or disguise. The next time you find yourself unsure about someone or something, take a moment to step back from the words and actions and focus on how you feel. This internal reaction is a powerful guide to understanding the true nature of the situation or person.

Key Takeaways

1. **Energy Speaks Volumes**: Trust the energy you feel in situations and around people. It often reveals more than words or appearances ever can.
2. **Surface vs. Depth**: Don't be fooled by polished surfaces or sweet talk. The true essence of a person or situation is often hidden beneath a well-crafted exterior.
3. **Authenticity Over Facades:** Recognize that energy is an unchangeable factor that cannot be easily manipulated. It's a reliable indicator of the underlying reality.

Actionable Tips

- **Tune Into Your Feelings.** Pay close attention to your emotional responses when interacting with people or entering new environments. This instinctive reaction can provide crucial insights.
- **Observe the Underlying Vibe.** When assessing a place or situation, look beyond the surface. Notice the subtle energy shifts and how they align with your gut feelings.
- **Reflect and evaluate.** Regularly evaluate whether the energy you perceive aligns with the actions and words of those around you. Discrepancies may signal deeper issues or truths.

29

Embrace Your Inner Black Sheep

Recently, I had the privilege of attending a private event at YouTube and Google's head office in London. Google, being the tech giant it is, outdid itself in creating an environment that is as innovative and inspiring as you'd expect. The head office itself was a marvel of modern design, a perfect backdrop for an event that was all about pushing boundaries and thinking differently.

The highlight of the day was a talk by Kirk Valis. For those who don't know, Kirk is a guru in the realm of creative problem-solving. He's worked with top companies in Silicon Valley through to sporting giants like the England national football team. Let me tell you, his insights were nothing short of eye-opening. One concept he discussed particularly resonated with me: the idea of "sheep mentality" versus being a "black sheep."

Imagine this: a pen full of sheep, all moving in unison, following each other without a second thought. This is what Kirk referred to as the "sheep mentality." It's the epitome of conformist behaviour, where everyone follows the herd, sticking to what's familiar and safe. People with this mindset rarely question the status quo; they simply follow along, doing things the way they've always been done. It's comfortable, predictable and oh-so-easy.

What about those who break away from the herd? These are the black sheep—the rebels, the innovators, the ones who question everything. They're the ones who see the world differently and aren't afraid to voice their unique perspectives, even if it means facing criticism or isolation. Being a black sheep isn't about being contrary for the sake of it; it's about challenging norms and daring to forge a new path.

In the synchronicity of life, I had had a moment that morning that perfectly illustrated this concept. I came across a message in a group chat that I found deeply inappropriate. It wasn't just an offhand comment; it was something that crossed boundaries and struck a nerve with me. I had a choice: stay silent and blend in with the crowd, or speak up and challenge what I saw as unacceptable.

I chose to speak up. It wasn't easy, and yes, it stirred up some unease. Yet in that moment, I realised that I wasn't just reacting to a single comment; I was embodying the black sheep mentality. I was choosing to stand up for my values and integrity, even if it meant facing backlash.

The key takeaway from Kirk's talk—and my own experience—is that the status quo is often just a comfortable illusion. If you want to make a difference, if you want to be a true innovator, you have to be willing to step outside of the herd. You have to be prepared for discomfort and dissent, because that's where real growth and progress happens.

Key Takeaways

1. **Question Everything**: Embrace the black sheep mentality by constantly challenging norms and questioning the status quo. Don't just follow the crowd—think critically about why things are done the way they are and whether there's a better way.
2. **Embrace Discomfort:** Innovation often comes with discomfort. If an idea or action makes you "uncomfortably excited," it's a sign you're on the right track. Don't shy away from it; lean into it and see where it takes you.
3. **Stand Up for Your Values:** When faced with situations that clash with your personal values, don't be afraid to speak up. Being true to yourself and your beliefs is more important than fitting in or avoiding conflict.

Actionable Tips

- **Reflect on Conformity.** Take a moment to evaluate areas of your life where you might be conforming out of habit or fear. Identify at least one area where you can challenge the norm and try a new approach.
- **Create a Discomfort Checklist.** For any new idea or project, assess whether it makes you feel uncomfortably excited. Use this as a gauge to determine if you're on the right path for innovation and growth.
- **Practise Speaking Up.** Start with small, manageable situations where you can practise voicing your concerns or alternative perspectives. Build your confidence in expressing your values and opinions, even when it feels uncomfortable.

30

The Three As: Navigating Life with Appreciation, Advice and Attraction

In life, the lessons we learn often come from unexpected places and the most impactful ones frequently arise from our interactions with others. I've recently encountered a series of experiences that have given me profound insights into what I call "The Three As": Appreciation, Advice and Attraction. These three aspects have not only shaped my life but also offered valuable lessons that can resonate with anyone, no matter where you are in the world.

1. Appreciation: The Foundation of Fulfillment

Appreciation is a powerful force that can make or break our experience in any environment, especially in the workplace. I recently experienced appreciation on both ends of the spectrum—feeling deeply valued in one instance and utterly overlooked in another.

I had the privilege of attending an exclusive event at Google's head office in London, organised by YouTube. The event was a revelation in how much an organisation can value and appreciate its employees and creators. The atmosphere at Google was one of mutual respect, where every individual's contribution was acknowledged and celebrated. It was a stark contrast to my own experience of working in South Italy, where I've often felt undervalued despite my efforts and achievements over the past six years.

Reflecting on this disparity, I realised that appreciation is not just a nicety—it's a vital component of motivation and productivity. When employees feel appreciated, they are more likely to be engaged, productive and loyal. On the other hand, a lack of appreciation can lead to resentment, disengagement and ultimately, a decline in the quality of work.

Appreciation also extends beyond the workplace. In our personal lives too, appreciation fosters growth and positivity. It's easy to overlook the small things, but when we take the time to genuinely appreciate our surroundings, our experiences and the people in our lives, we create a foundation for happiness and fulfillment. My new puppy, Tina, has been a constant reminder of this. Watching her discover the world with fresh eyes has made me more present and appreciative of the simple joys in life.

Ultimately, whether in our careers or personal lives, appreciation is the seed from which greater things grow. It's something we should all strive to give and receive more of.

2. Advice: The Double-Edged Sword

Advice is another common element of our interactions with others, but it can be a double-edged sword.

As a content creator, I'm no stranger to receiving feedback on my work. A few weeks ago, a fellow creator left a comment on one of my YouTube videos, offering unsolicited advice on how I could improve my channel. The advice was well-intended on the surface, but as I delved deeper, I realised there was more to consider.

The person who offered the advice had a channel with far more subscribers than mine, but when I checked her content, I noticed that her engagement was low, her videos had fewer views than mine and her thumbnails needed improvement. It struck me that despite her seemingly impressive subscriber count, her channel wasn't as successful as she implied. This experience underscored an important lesson: not all advice is worth taking, especially when it comes from someone who hasn't achieved what you aspire to.

We often receive advice from all corners—family, friends, colleagues and even strangers - but before accepting it, we need to consider the source. Is this person living the life we want? Have they walked in our shoes and achieved what we desire? If not, their advice might be more reflective of their own insecurities or unfulfilled dreams than of what's best for us.

There's also the fact that unsolicited advice can sometimes be more about the giver's need to assert themselves rather than genuinely helping others. It's crucial to discern whether the advice aligns with our goals and values or if it's merely a distraction. The takeaway here is simple:

be selective about whose advice you listen to and focus on following the guidance of those who have truly walked the path you wish to take.

3. Attraction: The Power of Energy and Connection

The third A—Attraction—is perhaps the most subtle but equally powerful. Attraction isn't just about physical or romantic appeal; it's about the energy we emit and the connections we forge with others.

There's a saying that's been on my mind lately: "a moth to a flame." Just as moths are drawn to light, people are drawn to energy. Each of us has an aura, an energy that we project into the world and this energy can attract or repel others. Some people have a magnetic aura that draws others in, while others may find that their energy pushes people away.

In recent months, I've observed how some relationships in my life have shifted. People who were once close have become distant and those who were once enthusiastic about my work have grown lukewarm. It reminded me of the transient nature of attraction and relationships. Just as seasons change, so do the people in our lives. Some connections are meant to be fleeting, while others endure. However every interaction, whether long-lasting or brief, teaches us something valuable.

It's important to understand why we're attracted to certain people or opportunities. Are we drawn to them for genuine connection and mutual growth, or are we seeking something more superficial? Similarly, why are others attracted to us? Are they genuinely interested in who we are, or are they looking to benefit from our success?

Being mindful of these dynamics helps us foster more meaningful connections and avoid the pitfalls of superficial relationships. In a world full of distractions and fleeting interests, nurturing deep, authentic relationships is a rarity but also a necessity for a fulfilling life.

The Three As—Appreciation, Advice and Attraction—are interwoven into the fabric of our daily lives. They shape our experiences, influence our decisions and determine the quality of our relationships. By cultivating genuine appreciation, being discerning about the advice we take and understanding the dynamics of attraction, we can navigate life's challenges with greater wisdom and clarity.

Key Takeaways

1. **Appreciation is Essential for Fulfillment**: Whether in your professional or personal life, feeling appreciated fuels motivation, engagement and a sense of purpose. The absence of appreciation can lead to disengagement and dissatisfaction.
2. **Be Discerning with Advice**: Not all advice is beneficial. It's crucial to consider the source of advice and whether the person offering it has the experience or success you aspire to achieve. Align advice with your goals and values.
3. **Understand the Dynamics of Attraction**: Attraction isn't just about physical appeal; it's about the energy you emit and the connections you forge. Being mindful of who you attract and why helps you foster meaningful relationships.

Actionable Tips

- **Cultivate Appreciation in Your Environment:**
- In the Workplace: Regularly acknowledge the efforts of colleagues and team members, whether through formal recognition or a simple thank you. It builds a positive atmosphere and boosts morale.
- In your Personal Life: Take time to express gratitude to friends, family and loved ones. A handwritten note, a thoughtful message or verbal appreciation can deepen your relationships.
- **Evaluate the Advice You Receive:**
- Ask Critical Questions: Before acting on advice, consider the advisor's experience and whether their life aligns with your aspirations. Ask yourself if their guidance fits with your values and long-term goals.
- Seek Multiple Perspectives: Don't rely on just one source. Gather insights from various individuals with proven success in the areas you're focused on, to get a well-rounded perspective.
- **Be Mindful of Your Energy and Relationships:**
- Self-Reflection: Regularly assess the energy you're projecting. Are you positive, approachable, and authentic? Adjust your behaviour and mindset to attract the kind of relationships and opportunities you desire.
- Evaluate Connections: Periodically review your relationships. Identify which ones are mutually beneficial and which may be draining or superficial. Focus on nurturing connections that align with your values and contribute to your growth.

31

Expat or Immigrant?

As global mobility continues to rise, with millions of people relocating to new countries every year, the terms we use to describe these individuals have become a focal point of discussion. Among the most debated labels are "expat" and "immigrant." These words, while seemingly straightforward, carry with them a host of connotations, assumptions and biases that can shape perceptions, influence policies and impact personal identities.

To begin, it's important to understand the technical definitions of the terms "expat" and "immigrant." According to the Cambridge English Dictionary:

- An **expatriate** (or "expat") is "someone who does not live in their own country."
- An **immigrant** is "a person who has come to a different country in order to live there permanently."

At first glance, these definitions suggest that the two categories might overlap and indeed, many individuals could arguably fit into both. An expat is simply someone living outside their home country, without any indication of the permanence of their stay. An immigrant, however, is someone who has relocated with the intention of permanent settlement. The distinction then, seems to hinge on intent and duration, yet in practice, these definitions blur.

When I first moved to Italy in 2018, I naturally gravitated toward the label "expat." It was the term I encountered most frequently in online communities, news reports and social media discussions about people living abroad. I joined expat groups, contributed to forums and even launched my YouTube channel under the banner of "Life as an expat in Italy." It felt like the appropriate label—a title that described my new reality in a foreign country, filled with cultural exploration and adaptation.

However, as time passed and my connection to Italy deepened, the term "expat" began to feel insufficient. I wasn't just a visitor or someone temporarily working abroad; I was building a life here. I dealt with the same bureaucratic challenges as any local—navigating the complexities of health insurance and tax regulations. I realised that, by the dictionary definition, I was also an immigrant. This realisation was cemented when others began questioning my use of the term "expat," suggesting that I might better be described as an "immigrant".

This identity crisis led me to a deeper reflection: Why did the term "expat" feel more comfortable? Why did "immigrant" seem to carry a heavier, more complicated weight? The answers to these questions lie in the cultural connotations and societal biases associated with each term.

In many Western societies, the term "expat" is often reserved for individuals from wealthier, predominantly Western countries who move abroad for work, retirement or leisure. "Expats" are frequently perceived as privileged, financially independent and having the freedom to choose their new home without the pressures of economic necessity or political unrest. They are often seen as cosmopolitan, adventurous and culturally curious.

On the other hand, the term "immigrant" is more commonly associated with individuals from developing or less economically stable regions. "Immigrants" are often perceived as people fleeing hardship, seeking better opportunities for themselves and their families and struggling to integrate into their new societies. The word "immigrant" is frequently loaded with connotations of struggle, survival and at times, illegality—a stark contrast to the seemingly carefree lifestyle associated with "expats".

These biases are not rooted in the dictionary definitions but in societal perceptions and the ways in which the media and public frame these identities. The media often reinforces these stereotypes by selectively applying these labels. For example, we rarely hear the term "illegal expat," but "illegal immigrant" is a common phrase in discussions of immigration policy.

The media plays a significant role in shaping the public's understanding of who qualifies as an "expat" and who is deemed an "immigrant". News stories about Westerners retiring in Italy or Spain often describe these individuals as "expats", even though they have relocated permanently and, by definition, could also be considered "immigrants". Conversely, when discussing individuals from less affluent nations, the term "immigrant" is almost exclusively used, often in the context of economic migration or asylum seeking.

This selective labelling can have profound implications. By framing "expats" as privileged and "immigrants" as desperate, the media perpetuates a hierarchy of migration that is more reflective of global power dynamics than of the actual experiences of individuals moving across borders.

When we insist on categorising people as either "expats" or "immigrants", we risk oversimplifying complex human experiences and reinforcing harmful stereotypes. People's lives are not black and white and their reasons for moving to a new country are often a mix of personal choice, economic opportunity, family ties and sometimes, necessity.

For example, there are "immigrants" who, despite facing initial struggles, build successful businesses, contribute to their communities and thrive in their new environments. Similarly, there are "expats" who, despite their privilege, encounter significant challenges in adjusting to life abroad, from language barriers to cultural differences. These individuals defy the simplistic narratives that the labels "expat" and "immigrant" suggest.

As someone who identifies as both an "expat" and an "immigrant", I have come to appreciate the complexity of my own identity. I recognise the privilege I have in being able to choose to live in another country, but I also acknowledge the realities of my life as an "immigrant"—navigating the legal, social and cultural landscapes of a foreign country. This dual identity allows me to sit in a space that acknowledges both the freedom and the challenges of global mobility.

The next time someone tells you they are an "expat", it's worth pausing before reflexively labelling them as an "immigrant" or vice versa. Both labels can be true and both deserve respect. By embracing the full spectrum of migration experiences, we can move beyond simplistic categories and begin to see people as they truly are—individuals with unique stories, motivations and challenges.

In a world that increasingly values labels and categorisations, it is essential to remember that identity is often far more complex than the terms we use to describe it. The distinction between "expat" and "immigrant" may seem clear-cut on the surface, but it becomes much more nuanced when we consider the lived experiences of individuals. Whether one identifies as an "expat", an "immigrant" or both, what matters most is the recognition of their humanity, their experiences and the respect they deserve as members of a global community.

In the end, the labels we choose—or are given—should not limit our understanding of ourselves or others. Instead, they should serve as a starting point for deeper reflection on the diverse and dynamic ways in which people navigate life in a world without borders.

Key Takeaways

1. **Labels Carry Weight and Biases**: The terms "expat" and "immigrant" are often loaded with societal connotations that go beyond their dictionary definitions. "Expat" is frequently associated with privilege and choice, while "immigrant" is linked to struggle and necessity, reflecting broader cultural biases.
2. **Identity is Multifaceted:** Many people who move abroad can identify as both "expats" and "immigrants". It's important to recognise that these categories are not mutually exclusive and that an individual's experience can span both identities.
3. **The Media Influences Perceptions**: Media portrayal often

reinforces stereotypes by selectively applying the labels "expat" and "immigrant" based on nationality, socioeconomic status and race. This influences public perception and can perpetuate a hierarchy of migration.

Actionable Tips

- **Reflect on Your Own Labels**. If you live or plan to live abroad, take some time to consider how you identify and why. Are you more comfortable with one label over the other? Understanding the implications of these terms can help you better navigate your identity.
- **Challenge Stereotypes**. When discussing migration or reading about it in the media, question the language used. Why is someone being called an "expat" versus an "immigrant"? Challenge these stereotypes in conversations with others to promote a more nuanced understanding of global mobility.
- **Engage with Both Communities**. If you're living abroad, try to connect with both "expat" and "immigrant" communities. Engaging with a diverse range of perspectives will enrich your experience and help you understand the varied challenges and privileges associated with living in a new country.
- **Use Inclusive Language**. In your own communications, whether in social media, blogs or conversations, use language that acknowledges the complexity of people's experiences. Avoid using labels in a way that could reinforce stereotypes or diminish someone's lived experience.

32

The Few Who Do

I'm currently reading *Unlimited Power* by Tony Robbins and I have to say, this book is a revelation. It was written in the late 1980s, but the insights are just as relevant today as they were back then. It's one of those books that you can pick up at any point in your life and the principles inside will still resonate. The lessons in just the first few chapters alone have already impacted how I think about success, growth and life in general.

One of the biggest takeaways is this idea that success is not a destination—it's an ongoing process. Robbins explains that success isn't about reaching some specific goal and then kicking back. It's about continuously striving to be more, to do more, to evolve. This really struck a chord with me because it's the same philosophy I live by. Life isn't about staying at the same level forever. You've got to turn the volume up, crank it as high as it can go. Of course, there will be moments where you need to dial it back, but the core of life is growth. You're meant to keep moving, keep changing, keep striving to improve.

I've met so many people who allow their circumstances—where they live, what they do, the people around them—to hold them back. They use these things as excuses not to work on themselves. However I believe that in this day and age, there are *no* excuses. The internet gives you access to unlimited free resources—videos, articles, online courses—so even if you're stuck in a tiny town with no one around to inspire you, you can still grow.

Robbins also talks about the importance of "modelling." This is such a powerful concept. Essentially, you can reverse-engineer success by studying successful people. Success leaves clues. You don't have to reinvent the wheel; you just have to pay attention to what the people you admire are doing and adopt those same behaviours. What do they prioritise? What mindsets do they cultivate? How do they approach their work and their lives? When you start modelling the behaviours of successful people, you're already on your way to finding success for yourself.

Now, here's the kicker. There's a big difference between the few who actually do things and the many who just talk about it. You know the type—they have big dreams and grand ideas, but they never seem to follow through. It's all talk. The people who *actually* make things happen, they don't just dream about it. They take action. They get things done. How many times have you thought about starting something— maybe a business, a YouTube channel, moving to a new country—and then you didn't act on it? It's easy to fall into that trap of thinking about it but never doing it.

The thing is, action is the crux of everything. No matter how big your dream is, it won't become reality without work and without commitment. Sometimes this means going against the grain, doing things differently than the people around you. While others might be lounging on the beach or bingeing Netflix, you're putting in the hours to build something meaningful. It's not that you can't enjoy life, but you have to find that balance—between hard work, passion and enjoying the journey.

For me, that's why I've made the choice to cut out things that don't serve my growth. I don't even watch TV anymore, not because I'm in Italy and can't get the channels I used to, but because I simply don't miss it. Instead, I spend my time feeding my mind with inspiring content, whether it's a great book or an inspiring YouTube video. This is how I prime myself for success. It's not just about taking action—it's about setting myself up for continuous improvement.

Less talk, more action. That's what it all boils down to.

Key Takeaways

1. **Success is a continuous process of growth.** It's not about hitting one goal and stopping, it's about constantly evolving and improving, no matter where you are in life.
2. **Success leaves clues.** You don't have to invent your own path from scratch. Model the behaviours, mindsets and actions of successful people to find your own way to success.
3. **The few who do vs. the many who talk** . Most people dream, but only a few take real action. Be the person who acts, not just the person who talks.

Actionable Tips

- **Identify one area of your life to improve**. Choose something specific you want to work on and commit to learning more about it. Watch videos, read books and apply what you learn.
- **Find a role model and study them.** Whether it's a public figure, an author or someone in your life, find a successful person who inspires you and study their habits, mindset and work ethic.
- **Take one small action today.** Whatever your dream is—starting a business, moving to a new country, launching a project—do *one thing* today that brings you closer to that goal. It could be as small as sending an email or researching the first step, but the key is to take action.

33

Embracing Your Inner Compass

How many times have you heard someone say, "Listen to your gut"? It's a phrase that gets tossed around a lot, often dismissed as a vague notion or dismissed in favour of cold, hard logic. Let's pause and really think about it. How many moments in your life have you ignored that nagging inner voice, choosing instead to go with what seems more sensible on paper? How often have you found yourself regretting those decisions?

Recently, I've been diving deep into this very topic, reflecting on my own journey here in Italy. You see, there have been countless times when my gut instinct clashed with the more rational, logical choices. People around me often looked at my decisions with confusion or scepticism. They couldn't understand why I would choose a little-known city in South Italy over the bustling allure of Milan or the familiar comforts of London, for example.

Here's the thing: my move to Salerno wasn't based on any logical framework. It was about a feeling, an inexplicable connection that spoke to me in a language beyond reason. Guess what? It was the best decision I could have ever made.

Salerno is not a city that boasts the high-profile reputation of Milan. It's a place that tests you, challenges you and yes, it makes you grow in ways you didn't anticipate. I remember spending those initial four weeks there, immersed in the language and culture and feeling an undeniable pull towards this place. It wasn't rational, but it was right. Living in Salerno has been one of the most profound experiences of my life, providing growth and perspective I couldn't have gained anywhere else.

Sometimes, our intuition about a person is just as powerful as it is about places. I've found that my gut feelings about people, whether good or bad, are usually spot-on. It's a skill that's not always appreciated by those around you, especially if your instincts don't align with popular opinion. However if you learn to listen, you'll find that your inner compass is rarely wrong.

I recently saw a humorous clip online—a woman's face was unmistakably unimpressed while the text read, "POV: Your wife's face says it all." It resonated with me because it's exactly how I react to certain situations or people. My gut doesn't lie. It might not always align with what others think or what seems logical, but it's a vital tool for navigating life's choices.

Listen to your gut. Even when it defies logic or when others don't understand it. It's not always easy, and sometimes it feels like you're going against the grain. Trust me though, your gut has a way of guiding you towards what you need, not just what you want.

Key Takeaways

1. **Trust Your Intuition:** Your gut feeling is more than just a fleeting thought—it's a deep, internal guide. Even if it doesn't make sense on paper, give it the consideration it deserves.
2. **Embrace the Challenges**: Sometimes, the best choices lead to unexpected challenges. Embrace these tests as opportunities for growth, just like I did with my move to Salerno.
3. **Be Honest with Yourself:** Whether it's about a place or a person, your gut feelings are there for a reason. Trust them, even if they go against the grain or the opinions of others.

Actionable Tips

- **Pause and Reflect.** When making decisions, take a moment to sit with your feelings. Notice any physical sensations—tension, relaxation or unease—and consider how they might be guiding you.
- **Keep a Journal.** Document your gut feelings and the outcomes of your decisions. Over time, you'll see patterns and gain more confidence in trusting your instincts.
- **Practise Mindfulness.** Engage in mindfulness practices to better connect with your inner self. This helps in distinguishing between genuine intuition and anxiety or fear.

34

You Just Can't Help Some People

I've come to a conclusion that's probably long overdue: you can't help everyone. It's something we don't like to admit to ourselves, especially when we're naturally inclined to care or feel responsible for others. Recently though, life has reminded me of a truth I can't ignore anymore. Some people are simply beyond help - not because they're incapable - but because they refuse to be helped.

Let me tell you what happened.

This year was the 400th-year celebration of the Patron Saint of Palermo - Santa Rosalia. Every year on 14th and 15th July, the city comes alive with parades, fireworks and religious processions to honour its Patron Saint. This year was particularly special. The float they created was more stunning than ever and the fireworks danced across the sky for a full hour. The entire city felt the weight of its history in those celebrations.

However, what should have been a moment of pride turned into something else for me.

I didn't attend the main parade on the 14th, but I made it to the quieter procession the following day. The float was magnificent, standing there in all its glory by the sea. What struck me, though, wasn't the float's beauty—it was the behaviour of the people around it. Despite the tall metal railings meant to protect the float, I saw people clambering all over it like it was a playground. At first, I thought maybe it was intentional. Maybe, because it was the 400th year, they'd opened it up to the public. As I got closer though, I realised that wasn't the case. People had taken it upon themselves to open the gates and climb on the float, using it as a mere prop for selfies.

No police. No security. Just blatant disrespect.

These are the same people who constantly complain about how the city doesn't spend its money wisely—about potholes, the state of the streets and the cleanliness of public spaces. Yet here they were, disrespecting something that countless people had spent months creating, something that represents the heart of the city's cultural heritage. It was the ultimate irony. How can you expect your city to be better when you don't even respect what you have?

It made me realise something: no amount of money or city planning will fix a place where the people don't care about it. You can throw millions at infrastructure, at cleaning crews, at beautifying projects, but if the residents don't take responsibility, it's pointless.

That wasn't the only instance though that brought me to this conclusion. As an English teacher here in Italy, I face another, albeit less dramatic, form of resistance to help. Teaching is an exercise in patience and understanding, yet it often feels like a battle against ego and complacency. Some students, for example, insist on positioning themselves at levels far beyond their grasp, unwilling to accept the basic truths about their current abilities. They want the prestige of higher levels without laying the necessary groundwork. Their resistance to acknowledging their starting point not only hampers their progress but also leads to frustration when they fail to meet their goals.

It's hard not to get discouraged when you're trying to guide someone toward growth, but they're too busy convincing themselves they've already arrived.

I've come to realise that despite my best efforts, there will always be those who are more interested in maintaining their illusions of competence rather than embracing genuine growth. This is not just a student issue; it's a broader human condition. People often resist change, not because they are incapable but because their egos prevent them from seeing the necessity of moving backwards to move forwards.

In both the public's disrespect for communal celebrations and students' denial of their learning needs, I've learnt a crucial lesson: some things are beyond my control. I can strive to teach, guide and contribute positively, but ultimately, I must accept that not everyone will respond as hoped. This acceptance isn't about giving up; rather, it's about understanding my limits and focusing on what I can influence while letting go of what I cannot.

I embrace the imperfections of the world around me and the individuals within it. I choose to continue working with integrity, to respect the efforts of others and to focus on my own growth and contributions. Sometimes, the best we can do is lead by example and let the universe take care of the rest.

Key Takeaways

1. **Personal responsibility is non-negotiable**: Whether it's taking care of your surroundings or taking ownership of your learning, real progress only happens when people are accountable for their actions.
2. **Ego blocks growth**: The moment we convince ourselves we're better than we actually are is the moment we halt our progress. To grow, we need to be humble and accept where we are.
3. **You can't help everyone**: Some people aren't ready for help. Recognise when to step back and let them face the consequences of their actions. This isn't giving up—it's respecting their journey.

Actionable Tips

- **Set boundaries when helping others**. You can guide, you can support, but ultimately, people have to do the work themselves. Stop pouring energy into situations where your help isn't appreciated or acted upon. Learn to recognise when it's time to step back.
- **Encourage accountability**. Whether it's at work, in your community or in your personal life, gently remind those around you that they have a role to play in the world they want to see. Start with small acts of respect—whether that's not littering in your neighbourhood or admitting you need to work on your skills.
- **Focus on your integrity, not the outcome.** You can't control how others behave, but you can control how you show up. Do your best from a place of integrity and let go of the need to fix things for people who don't want to be fixed. Focus on doing *your* part well and let the rest take care of itself.

35

The Rush to Judgement

When I publish a video on YouTube, I can almost always tell who's really watching and who's just skimming. It's become second nature. Analytics are part of it, sure, but I also get a pretty good sense from the comments. You can almost divide the comments into two camps: those who've taken their time to watch the full video, absorbing the full message and those who've caught just a piece of it and jumped to conclusions.

Take, for example, a video series I did last year. The topic was simple enough—Sicily. I made two videos, one with seven reasons to visit Sicily and one with seven reasons not to visit Sicily. Now, human nature being what it is, the "seven reasons not to" video performed way better than the positive one. That's just how we're wired. What was fascinating to me though were the reactions. Those who watched both videos—the complete series—really appreciated the balance I was aiming for. They understood that my goal was to paint a full picture, both the good and the challenging aspects of life in Sicily.

Then there were the other comments. You know, the ones where it was obvious the person had barely scratched the surface before they decided to air their opinions. These comments were often critical and missed the point entirely. I would read them and think, "You just didn't get it." They hadn't watched long enough to understand the full context, but that didn't stop them from firing off their thoughts.

It's really interesting, isn't it? Watching people—myself included at times—rush to judgement without fully understanding a situation. This habit of forming an opinion based on a snippet of information, rather than taking the time to gather the full facts. It's something we see everywhere these days. We live in a time where immediacy is valued over thoroughness. There's a sense of urgency—an unspoken rule that everything needs to happen right now. Get things done. Move fast. Comment quickly. Post immediately. The irony is that, in our rush to be heard, we often miss the point entirely.

It reminds me of something I've been reading in Anthony Robbins' book, *Unlimited Power*. Robbins talks about how we can control our minds, how we don't have to let our initial reactions dictate our actions. I see this playing out in real life, all the time. People react impulsively to something that triggers them, instead of taking a moment, stepping back and thinking through their response.

Which brings me to an analogy I find really fitting because as I write this, the Olympics are just around the corner. Picture an athlete preparing for the long jump. They don't just leap blindly from the edge of the pit, right? No, they take a long run-up. They gather momentum, build up speed and only when they've reached the right point do they make their jump. That's how they achieve distance. Those who comment after watching just a few minutes of my videos? They're like people who just stand at the edge of the sand pit, jump without the run-up and expect to go far. Spoiler alert: they don't.

It's such an apt metaphor for how we live our lives. We make hasty decisions, reacting quickly without all the information and then wonder why we didn't go as far as we wanted. Sometimes we need to take our time, gather our thoughts and be intentional about our actions before we leap.

Now, I'm not saying we should always take things slowly. In fact, there are times when action needs to be swift and decisive. The Italian philosophy of *piano piano*—slowly, slowly—isn't something I always subscribe to. There are moments in life when you need to move fast to seize an opportunity or make a change. However there are also moments when it pays to slow down, reflect and take your time to fully understand a situation before reacting.

This is where the *piano, piano* mindset becomes valuable. Not everything in life needs to be done in an instant. Some things require reflection. They require thought. They require patience.

There are some moments that simply require you to take your time.

Key Takeaways

1. **Patience Leads to Clarity**: Taking time to fully understand a situation before forming an opinion allows you to gain a more balanced and accurate perspective. Rushing often leads to misunderstandings and unnecessary criticism.
2. **Impulsive Reactions Limit Success**: Jumping to conclusions without gathering all the facts is like trying to leap without a proper

run-up—you won't go as far. Measured actions, based on full understanding, lead to better results.

3. **The Balance Between Action and Reflection**: While quick actions can be necessary in some cases, reflection and patience are vital in others. Knowing when to act quickly and when to slow down can make the difference between success and regret.

Actionable Tips

- **Pause Before Reacting.** When you feel triggered by something—whether it's a comment, a video or a situation—take a moment before responding. Count to ten, breathe or take a break to gather your thoughts.
- **Watch or Read in Full Before Commenting**. Whether it's an article, a video or a conversation, commit to consuming the entire content before forming an opinion. This will ensure you respond with a well-rounded perspective.
- **Adopt a "Run-Up" Mentality.** When faced with a decision, gather as much information as possible before making a move. Treat it like preparing for a long jump—build momentum with knowledge before you leap into action.
- **Practise the 24-Hour Rule.** If you're unsure about a decision or response, give yourself 24 hours to think about it. This method allows emotions to settle and helps you approach situations with a clearer mind.
- **Balance Fast Action with Thoughtful Reflection.** Recognise when swift action is needed, but for important decisions or emotional situations, give yourself permission to slow down.

36

The Mouldy Strawberry

You've probably heard the famous quote about being the average of the five people you spend the most time with. It's one of those sayings that we often recite without fully grasping its depth. Yet, the truth behind it is incredibly profound and often underestimated. Recently, a friend of mine shared an analogy that perfectly encapsulates this concept and it's one that I think you'll appreciate.

Imagine two strawberries: one is fresh, ripe and bursting with flavour and the other is mouldy and rotten. If you keep the mouldy strawberry close to the fresh one for long enough, the mould will eventually spread, corrupting the once-juicy berry. This simple, yet vivid image is an excellent metaphor for the impact of the people around us on our own lives.

Spending time with negative, toxic individuals is like placing that mouldy strawberry next to the fresh one. Their negativity, lack of direction and low energy can gradually infect you, making you feel less vibrant and more disheartened. Even if you believe you have a strong mindset and a clear direction, the influence of those around you can subtly, but significantly, alter your course.

On the flip side, being in the company of high-vibe, positive people who inspire and uplift you can transform your outlook and energy. I've experienced this firsthand: after spending time with individuals who are driven, passionate and optimistic, I've always left feeling like I could conquer the world. This kind of environment makes your dreams feel attainable and fuels you with the motivation to make them a reality.

There's a stark contrast between the two types of environments. One is filled with complaints and inertia, a comfort zone of lack where people are stuck in the same old patterns, unwilling to change or strive for more. You've probably been there—surrounded by those who are perpetually dissatisfied yet make no effort to improve their situation. This can be draining and you may feel a sense of heaviness and stagnation just from being around them.

The other environment contains an infectious energy of possibility, resourcefulness and the acute knowledge that we create our own realities. Trust me, this environment feels totally different.

Modern society, especially with social media, often glorifies having a massive network of "friends" and followers. The blunt truth is though that not all connections are valuable. Quantity doesn't equate to quality. I've learnt that having a few deep, genuine relationships is far more rewarding than having countless superficial ones. It's about the quality of your interactions, not just the number of people you know.

In a world that promotes the illusion of popularity, I've found peace in embracing solitude when necessary and being selective about who is in my inner circle. I'd rather spend time alone than be surrounded by people who don't truly enrich my life. The rare, meaningful connections you make—those with people who genuinely lift you up and inspire you—are the ones to treasure. They are the ones which will help you grow, flourish and stay true to your authentic self.

If you consistently surround yourself with people who don't uplift you or encourage your growth, you risk becoming like them—mouldy and rotten. Conversely, if you make the effort to be around those who positively impact your life, you'll find yourself blossoming into the best version of yourself.

Key Takeaways

1. **Be Selective with Your Inner Circle**: Just like the strawberries, your environment and the people around you have a profound impact on your wellbeing. Choose to surround yourself with those who inspire and elevate you.
2. **Quality Over Quantity**: Focus on building deep, meaningful relationships rather than collecting a large number of superficial connections. The value of genuine connections far outweighs the fleeting satisfaction of popularity.
3. **Recognise the Impact of Negativity**: Spending time with negative individuals can subtly influence you in ways you might not immediately notice. Be aware of how such interactions affect your energy and mindset.

Actionable Tips

- **Evaluate Your Relationships**. Take a moment to assess the people you spend the most time with. Identify who brings positivity and inspiration into your life and who drains your energy. Consider making changes if necessary.
- **Seek Out Uplifting Environments**. Actively look for opportunities to engage with high-energy, positive individuals. Attend events, join groups or participate in activities where you're likely to meet people who align with your values and aspirations.
- **Set Boundaries with Negative Influences**. If you have to interact with negative people, set clear boundaries to protect your own well-being. Limit your exposure and focus on maintaining a positive mindset despite external influences.

37

Embracing the Season of Introspection

Whenever we find ourselves deep in the throes of Mercury Retrograde, it's impossible not to feel the shift in energy around us. This particular season, more than any other, demands our attention—not just to the world outside but to the world within. It's a time when the universe subtly nudges us to turn inward, to slow down and to give ourselves permission to reflect. Although Mercury Retrograde often gets a bad rap for the disruptions it can bring to communication, travel plans and technology, I believe it holds a far greater opportunity for growth and self-discovery.

This is a time when introspection becomes a powerful tool—a mirror that allows us to see the patterns in our thoughts, the ways we process our emotions and the paths we've chosen to walk. Personally, I've been feeling this energy intensely this year.

Normally, I'm the type of person who thrives on productivity. I'm up at 5 a.m, ready to tackle the day with a morning routine that sets the tone for everything that follows. It's something I've done religiously, even before the arrival of our puppy Tina. My days are normally a whirlwind of activity—work, content creation and all the little things that bring me joy. This summer though, something shifted.

As the sun grew hotter and the days longer, I found my energy depleting in a way I hadn't expected. Suddenly, the routine that once fueled me felt like a burden. The 5 a.m. wake-ups that had been my anchor now felt impossible and the drive to accomplish everything on my list waned. It was unsettling at first. For someone who thrives on maximising every moment, this sudden lethargy felt alien to me.

Instead of forcing myself to push through though, I decided to do something I hadn't allowed myself to do in a long time: I listened to my body.

I began to realise that it was okay for my routine to change with the seasons. It was okay if I had more energy at dusk rather than at dawn and if the heat of the day drained me to the point where I only did what was absolutely necessary. This acceptance wasn't easy—it's a constant battle to let go of the need to be productive every waking moment. However the more I leaned into this change, the more I understood the importance of listening inward.

We live in a world that glorifies the hustle, that tells us we must always be on the move, always working towards the next goal. During Mercury Retrograde, the universe gives us a rare opportunity to pause. It invites us to reflect on where we're headed, how we feel about our journey and what we might want to change when this season of introspection passes.

For me, this reflection has been deeply tied to my life here in Italy. I've been living in this beautiful country for six years at the time of writing and it's been a journey filled with incredible highs and challenging lows. Recently, I found myself focusing more on the negatives—on the frustrations that come with living in a city that, while stunning, isn't always easy. I realised that this negativity was clouding my perspective, making it harder for me to see the things I once loved about Palermo.

This awareness has sparked a desire in me to shift my focus. I want to retrain my mind to see the beauty in my surroundings and to refocus my energy on the positive. When we actively look for things to be grateful for, we naturally attract more of that goodness into our lives. It's a simple truth, but one we often forget in the rush of our daily routines.

As I continue this journey of introspection, I've also been reflecting on a quote I came across recently from Steven Bartlett. It was a powerful reminder that sometimes we're so focused on the future that we forget we're already living the dream we once had. This struck a chord with me. I've built a life here in Italy that, at one point, was nothing more than a dream - a seed of inspiration that I nurtured into reality - yet how often do I stop to appreciate that?

We don't spend enough time reflecting on our journeys, on how far we've come and on the dreams we've realised. This season has shown me that I need to change that.

Taking time to disconnect, to be slow and steady, is something I'm learning to embrace more fully. I've realised that if we don't take these moments to listen to ourselves, to really think about where we're going and how we feel, we risk burning out. We risk losing the passion and joy that once lit us up. I don't want that for myself or for anyone reading this.

As humans, we're not designed to be in a constant state of hustle. We're meant to ebb and flow with the seasons, to adjust our pace according to the energy we have and the demands of our environment. Here in Italy, the summer heat is oppressive and trying to maintain the same level of productivity as I do in cooler months only leads to exhaustion. So, I'm learning to let go of the idea that my routine has to be rigid. I'm learning to embrace the slower energy of the season, to reflect on where I am and to appreciate the life I've built.

I encourage you to do the same.

Key Takeaways

1. **Listen to Your Body**: Just as the seasons change, so do our energy levels. It's important to adjust your routine based on how you feel, rather than forcing yourself to adhere to rigid schedules.
2. **Shift Your Focus to Gratitude:** When you find yourself dwelling on the negatives, consciously shift your attention to the positives. A daily gratitude practice can help reframe your perspective and attract more positivity into your life.
3. **Embrace the Season of Reflection:** Mercury Retrograde is the perfect time to pause and reflect on your journey. Use this period to think deeply about where you're headed, how you feel about your progress and what changes you might want to make.

Actionable Tips

- **Adjust Your Routine.** Take note of when you have the most energy and plan your day around that. If you feel more active in the evening, shift some of your tasks to later in the day.
- **Start a Gratitude Journal.** Each day, write down at least one thing you're grateful for. This can be as simple as a moment of peace or a beautiful view. Over time, you'll find it easier to focus on the positive aspects of your life.
- **Schedule Downtime.** Actively plan time for rest and reflection, especially during periods of high stress or significant astrological events like Mercury Retrograde. Use this time to disconnect from work and reconnect with yourself.
- **Reevaluate Your Goals.** Use the introspective energy of Mercury Retrograde to review your goals and aspirations. Are they still aligned with what you want? Are there changes you need to make?
- **Practise Mindful Reflection.** Spend a few minutes each day meditating or simply sitting quietly, allowing your thoughts to come and go without judgement. This can help you gain clarity and insight into your emotions and life direction.

38

The Dilemma of Authenticity

Recently I read a comment on my YouTube channel that left me questioning a fundamental aspect of my content: authenticity. Now, if you've followed me for a while, you know that I've always prided myself on being real—raw, even—about my experiences living in South Italy. As I read through the comment though, a question began to form in my mind: Can you be too authentic?

I've always approached my content with the mindset that honesty is the best policy. Life here in South Italy isn't always the romanticised dream that films and travel brochures would have you believe. Yes, there's stunning beauty, rich history and an incredible culture, but there are also challenges—real, everyday struggles that aren't as picturesque. That's what I share with you on my channel. I don't sugarcoat things; I tell it like it is. Yet, recently, I've noticed that my authenticity doesn't always sit well with everyone.

This comment in particular was from someone who, after watching a video about the reality of life in Palermo, had decided to skip visiting the city. That's when I started to worry. Was I inadvertently discouraging

168

people from exploring places that, despite their flaws, have so much to offer? It wasn't my intention to steer anyone away; I just wanted to prepare people to approach their visit with eyes wide open. However, maybe, in my effort to be transparent I was actually crossing a line. Was I really being too authentic?

Let's talk about what authenticity means, especially in the context of sharing your life experiences. We're often told to be true to ourselves, to express our genuine feelings and to live in alignment with our values. Why is it though that when we do this, it can sometimes trigger negative reactions from others? It's a strange paradox, isn't it? The very thing we're encouraged to embrace can actually make others uncomfortable.

I started to dig deeper into this idea of being "too authentic." It made me reflect on why I share what I do. The reality is, I'm not trying to deter anyone from visiting South Italy or anywhere else. Instead, I want people to come here prepared, to have a realistic understanding of the place, so that they can fully appreciate it. Let's be honest, no place in the world is perfect. Every city, every town, has its good points and its bad points. If you know what to expect, you're more likely to enjoy your experience, even if it's not the fairytale version you might have imagined.

Take Naples, for example. It's a city that often gets a bad rap. I've seen countless posts in expat groups and on social media asking, "Is it safe to visit Naples?" People have these preconceived notions about the city, usually based on sensationalism or second-hand accounts.

Here's the thing: any city can be safe or unsafe, depending on how you navigate it. As a former Police Officer, I can tell you that a lot of safety comes down to common sense—watching your belongings, being aware of your surroundings and doing a bit of research before you arrive. Sure, there are risks, but those exist everywhere. The key is to be prepared, not scared.

Reflecting on all of this, I realised that authenticity isn't about sugar-coating reality to make it more palatable. It's about presenting life as it is, with all its imperfections. Yes, some people might be put off by the truth, but that doesn't mean I should hold back. In fact, the more I think about it, the more I believe that authenticity is what gives depth and meaning to our experiences. When you truly understand a place—its heart and its soul—you connect with it on a much deeper level than if you only saw its polished, pristine surface.

So can you be too authentic? I don't think so. What I've come to realise is that authenticity isn't about controlling how others react to your truth. It's about being true to yourself, even when it's uncomfortable. You see, no matter what you say or how you say it, there will always be people who disagree, who find fault and who are triggered. For every person who's turned off by your honesty, there are others who find value in it, who appreciate the realness and who benefit from your perspective.

In the end, it's those people I choose to focus on. The ones who come to my channel not just for the picturesque views of South Italy, but for a real understanding of what life here is truly like. They're the ones who will visit Palermo, not because it's perfect, but because they're intrigued by its complexity and its authenticity. That to me, is worth any negative reaction my content might provoke.

Key Takeaways

1. **Authenticity Isn't About Being Perfect**: It's about being real, even when that means showing the less-than-perfect sides of life. This honesty allows others to connect with the truth, rather than an illusion.
2. **You Can't Control Others' Reactions**: No matter how carefully you present your truth, some people will always be triggered or put off. That's okay. What matters is staying true to your message and your experience.
3. **Preparedness Enhances Experience**: Authenticity, especially when it includes the negatives, isn't about deterring people. It's about preparing them for a richer, more nuanced experience.

Actionable Tips

- **Reflect Before Sharing**. Before you share an honest experience, ask yourself what your intention is. If it's to inform and prepare, then share it confidently, knowing that you're helping others approach a situation with realistic expectations.
- **Embrace Criticism Constructively.** When you receive negative feedback, use it as an opportunity to reflect on your approach, but don't let it silence your authenticity. Remember, not everyone will see things the way you do—and that's okay.
- **Balance Your Narrative.** While it's important to be honest about the challenges, don't forget to highlight the positives too. This balanced approach ensures that your audience gets a full picture, helping them make informed decisions.
- **Engage with Your Audience**. Open up a dialogue with your

viewers or readers. Encourage them to share their own experiences and perspectives, fostering a community where diverse opinions are respected and valued.

- **Stay True to Your Purpose**. Always remember why you started sharing in the first place. Whether it's to inform, educate or simply connect, let that purpose guide your content and don't be afraid to show the world who you really are.

39

The Power of Stopping

A recent break—a rare moment of complete disconnect - filled me with a sense of clarity and creative energy I hadn't felt in ages. It's funny, isn't it? The very act of stopping can feel so counterintuitive when you're used to constantly going. We're conditioned to believe that slowing down is akin to failure, that progress only comes from relentless action. What if I told you that stopping, really stopping, can be your most powerful tool for momentum?

During this break, I didn't pre-record my usual podcast episode. I didn't force myself to churn out content just to meet a schedule. Instead, I paused. I chose to hit the reset button, to fully immerse myself in the present moment and it turned out to be one of the most productive decisions I've made in a long time.

In that quiet, away from the noise of daily tasks, something profound happened. I rediscovered the paradox of stopping. In halting my routine, I gained the perspective I'd been missing. Instead of pushing forward blindly, I found a natural flow—a creative energy that came effortlessly. It's as though by stepping back, I allowed my mind to refuel, recalibrate and align myself with what I truly wanted to create.

After several days of rest, I suddenly found myself in a creative surge. Toward the end of the week, I redesigned my entire website in just a day and a half. The energy was there, the vision was clear and the execution felt natural. That's the paradox I'm talking about. By stepping back, I moved forward in ways that felt authentic and aligned. I didn't just push through for the sake of pushing through—I stopped, reflected and as a result, created something better.

It wasn't just about the website. It was about the understanding that stopping isn't a setback. It's a strategy. More than that, it's necessary. If you're feeling burnt out, running on fumes or unsure of your direction, the answer isn't to keep grinding. The answer is to stop. Stop and let yourself breathe. In that space, you'll find clarity, direction and maybe even a breakthrough.

Just as I was basking in the renewal of my break, I was met with a stark reminder of how fragile life truly is. Toward the end of that week, we heard tragic news—an unexpected storm hit the coast of Porticello, Sicily, sinking a boat and claiming multiple lives. The weather had been perfect for weeks and then, in the blink of an eye, everything changed. Lives were lost in a matter of moments.

This tragedy shook me. It reminded me how life can be upended at any moment, how quickly things can shift beyond our control. We often get so wrapped up in the day-to-day, in the pursuit of goals, in the accumulation of things, that we forget just how fragile our existence is. Nature, in her unpredictability, doesn't let us forget for long. In those moments of chaos—whether it's a storm, an earthquake or simply an unexpected life event—we're reminded that we're not in control. That's why it's so important to truly live.

This news made me pause and reflect. Am I living the way I want to? Am I appreciating the moments that matter? Am I taking the time to invest in what really fulfils me, or am I caught up in the materialistic chase that so many of us fall into?

I realised how much we take for granted. We rush through life, always thinking about the next milestone, the next achievement, and we forget to savour the present. Life is short and it's fragile. We don't know what tomorrow holds and we certainly can't plan for everything. So, shouldn't we make the most of today? Shouldn't we take more risks, live more fully and appreciate the simple moments that make life beautiful?

In the wake of this tragedy, I also started thinking about how we treat our world. Nature always reminds us who's really in charge but how often do we truly respect her? Here in Palermo, the neglect of the environment is staggering. There's so much rubbish, so much disregard for the natural beauty that surrounds us and it saddens me. How can we expect to thrive as a species if we don't even care for the world we live in?

The truth is, the way we treat the environment reflects how we treat ourselves. If we're careless with our surroundings, it's likely we're being careless with our own lives too. We need to nurture both. We need to live with more awareness—not just of the planet, but of our own purpose and well-being.

So, let this be a reminder to you, as it has been to me: Appreciate your life. Stop when you need to. Reflect on what truly matters. Take risks. Don't wait for life to slow down or for the perfect moment, because that moment may never come. The only thing we know for sure is that we have right now and it's our responsibility to make the most of it.

Key Takeaways

1. **The Paradox of Stopping**: Sometimes, stopping can lead to more progress than continuing to push forward. By pausing, you gain clarity, refocus your energy and create with greater purpose.
2. **Life's Fragility Is a Reminder:** Life can change in an instant. Tragedies, like the boat accident in Sicily, remind us to appreciate the present moment and not take anything for granted.
3. **Respect for Nature and Self:** How we treat the environment reflects how we treat ourselves. We need to care for both, as neglecting one will eventually harm the other.

Actionable Tips

- **Schedule Time to Pause.** Whether it's a weekend or just a day, set aside time to completely disconnect. No work, no goals—just be present. Use this time to reflect and recharge.
- **Practise Daily Gratitude.** At the end of each day, take a moment to think about three things you're grateful for. This will help you stay grounded in the present and appreciate the small moments.
- **Reconnect with Nature.** Spend time outdoors, even if it's just a short walk. It will remind you of the world beyond your to-do list and reconnect you with a greater sense of purpose.
- **Take One Risk a Week.** Whether it's starting a new project, reaching out to someone or trying something outside your comfort

zone, make a habit of taking small risks. Over time, this will help you live more fully.

40

Forty Lessons at Forty

Writing this, I stand on the cusp of forty one. Forty years on this Earth, forty chapters in this journey and what better way to wrap up this final chapter of Volume One, than by reflecting on the forty lessons I've gathered along the way? Synchronistic, isn't it?

These lessons have shaped my life, my time in Italy and my path going forward. So, here we go—forty lessons at forty.

1. Just Start

We often overthink, waiting for the perfect moment. Perfectionism doesn't exist. You'll never feel 100% ready. Take the first step, no matter how small and momentum will follow.

2. Inaction Equals Disinterest

If you're not taking action, maybe you don't actually care about it. Be honest with yourself about what you're truly passionate about and don't waste time on things that don't light your fire.

3. Stop Trying to Understand Everyone

People are complex. Fickle, even. Instead of trying to figure everyone out, accept that people will do what they do and focus on your life.

4. It's Never About You

When someone is rude or unkind, it's usually more about them than you. Don't take everything personally. You are not the centre of everyone's universe.

5. Don't Chase People

If someone is meant to be in your life, they'll stay. Don't waste energy on people who only come around when it's convenient for them.

6. Age Is a Self-Imposed Prison

We box ourselves into age-related expectations. Stop thinking you're "too old" for something. Age is just a number, and you're capable of anything at any time.

7. Karma Takes Care of Everything

What goes around, comes around. The universe always balances the scales. Trust that others will get what they deserve, good or bad.

8. A Qualification Doesn't Equal Intelligence

Degrees and diplomas don't define how smart or capable you are. Life experience and how you apply knowledge matter far more than pieces of paper.

9. What You Focus On Expands

If you focus on the negative, that's what you'll get more of. Focus on the things that bring you joy and watch how life changes.

10. You Create Your Reality

Yes, life throws curveballs, but your reactions shape your world. If something's not working, change it. You have more control than you think.

11. Comfort Zones Will Slowly Kill You

Staying comfortable for too long makes life dull. Take risks, challenge yourself and do things that scare you—it's how you grow.

12. Be Careful with Gossip

Gossip bonds people, but be cautious. The person who gossips to you will gossip about you. Keep your side of the street clean.

13. Mental Health is Serious

Don't play the mental health card to get attention. It's not a trend. Those who are truly struggling deserve our compassion, not our judgement.

14. Words Have Power

The words you use—about yourself, others and the world—shape your reality. Choose them carefully.

15. Check Your Ego

Sometimes your ego will try to protect you, but it might not always have the full picture. Be aware of when it's your ego talking versus your true self.

16. Problems Persist Until You Learn the Lesson

If you keep running into the same issue, it's because you haven't learnt what you need to from it. Pay attention to the patterns in your life.

17. You Can't Control Everything

Life has its own plans. Sometimes, despite your best efforts, things don't go as you hoped. Learn to let go and trust the process.

18. Speak Up

Whether it's about a bad service or something inappropriate someone said, don't be afraid to speak your mind. Silence is complicity.

19. Let Things Be

There are some things you simply cannot change. Stressing over them won't help. Let go of what's out of your control.

20. Express Gratitude

Gratitude changes everything. Even in the darkest moments, there is something to be thankful for and that gratitude will transform your perspective.

21. Be a "Do" Person, Not a "Try" Person

Trying is passive. Doing is active. Commit to your goals. You either do it or you don't—there's no middle ground.

22. Don't Be a Carbon Copy

Be yourself. Stop looking at what everyone else is doing and trying to mould yourself into someone else's image. Authenticity is where true happiness lies.

23. Feed Your Mind

Nourish your mind with things that inspire and uplift you—books, podcasts, nature—not just social media and entertainment.

24. You're Not Wrong in Thinking Differently

Even if it feels like the world is going one way, don't be afraid to go the other. The crowd isn't always right.

25. People Will Move On

Those who gossip or cause drama will move on to their next target once they lose interest in you. Don't give them your time or energy.

26. Comparison Reveals Your Desires

When you compare yourself to others, it often highlights what you truly want in life. Use it as a guide to pursue your own dreams—not as a way to bring yourself down.

27. Sacrifice Brings Rewards

If you want something, be prepared to make sacrifices. Nothing worthwhile comes without effort and some level of discomfort.

28. Script Your Life

You are the author of your story. Write it the way you want it to be. Visualise your dreams and take steps to make them real.

29. You Are Your Own Constant

No matter where life takes you, you are always with yourself. Learn to love and be kind to yourself—it's the most important relationship you'll ever have.

30. Social Media is Life's Best Edit

Remember, social media is a curated version of people's lives, not the whole story. Don't compare your reality to someone else's highlight reel.

31. Live in the Moment

Put down the phone. Stop documenting everything for likes and shares and just be present in your life. You'll experience it more fully.

32. Health is Everything

Without your health, none of the rest matters. Prioritise it, because it's the one thing money can't buy.

33. Learn to Read People

Words only tell part of the story. Learn to read body language, behaviour and energy to truly understand who someone is.

34. Be Careful with Your Circle

Surround yourself with people who lift you up, not those who bring drama or negativity into your life.

35. Your Energy Is Precious

Protect your energy like the valuable resource it is. Don't waste it on people or situations that drain you.

36. Don't Fear Change

Change is inevitable and it's often the very thing you need to grow. Embrace it instead of resisting.

37. Time is a Non-Renewable Resource

Your time is finite, so spend it wisely. Don't waste it on things or people who don't contribute to your happiness.

38. Take Ownership of Your Life

You are responsible for your life. No one else is going to live it for you. Own your decisions, mistakes and successes.

39. Celebrate the Small Wins

Don't wait for the big accomplishments to celebrate. Every step forward is progress. Recognise and appreciate it.

40. Gratitude, Always

This is where it all begins and ends. Every moment, good or bad, teaches you something. Be grateful for it all, because it shapes you into who you're meant to be.

About the Author

Claire Hearn is a former Police Officer and award-winning entrepreneur who decided in 2018, to change her life and relocate to Italy. She didn't know anyone there, didn't speak the language and had only visited the country twice before. Just eight months after making this decision, Claire packed up her suitcases and moved solo from London to the South of Italy, embarking on her very first expat experience. On paper it sounds completely bonkers but in reality Claire credits this as being the making of her.

In 2021, Claire started a YouTube channel and the *'Ms Britaly'* brand was born. Initially designed as a way to navigate the complexities of life in South Italy, Claire's content has gone on to help many people who are planning to visit or move to Italy. In 2023, Claire started her podcast, *Lessons From The Boot*, to share the personal growth and development that life in South Italy teaches her.

With her content, guides and products, Claire's aim is to continue to inspire lots more of you to discover the heart and soul of real Italy!

You can connect with me on:

- https://www.msbritaly.com
- https://www.youtube.com/msbritaly
- https://www.instagram.com/msbritaly
- https://podcasters.spotify.com/pod/show/ms-britaly

Also by Claire Hearn

Wake Up To Your Worth

In my very first book, I detail how I spent years of my life accepting the less than ideal behaviours and the breadcrumbs. I wasted chunks of my life on people who never appreciated me and I constantly looked to others to validate me. In short, I disempowered myself massively and I didn't love myself in the slightest.

Things changed when over Christmas of 2019 I had a breakdown, here in South Italy. From that place of feeling like I was underneath the rocks, a switch went off. In that moment I finally woke up to my worth. This book is here to help you wake up to yours.

www.ingramcontent.com/pod-product-compliance
Lightning Source LLC
Chambersburg PA
CBHW031127130726
47988CB00006B/2254